NATIONAL, LOCAL

NATIONAL, LOCAL, FAMILY: HISTORY FROM SOMERSET'S BISHOPS' REGISTERS, 1264–1559

Robert Dunning

SOMERSET RECORD SOCIETY

c/o Somerset Heritage Centre, Brunel Way, Norton Fitzwarren, Taunton, TA2 6SF
2022

© Robert Dunning
ISBN: 978 0 901732 50 7

Produced for the Somerset Record Society by 4word Ltd., Bristol

CONTENTS

References	vii
List of Illustrations	viii
Acknowledgements	ix
Introduction	1

Part One: The Registers
   Chapter I: How the Registers were made   5

Part Two: The People of the Registers
   Chapter II: Lay People and their Bishop   17
   Chapter III: The Clergy and their Parishes   26
   Chapter IV: Monasteries and Nunneries   36
   Chapter V: The Ordinary, the Devout and the Questioning   41
   Chapter VI: Marriage, Divorce and Family Problems   52
     Marriage Cases in the Registers   53
   Chapter VII: The Church Protects the Property of the Dead   52
     Wills and Testaments in the Registers   57

Part Three: Rural and Urban Landscapes
   Chapter VIII: The Countryside   66
   Chapter IX: Towns & Townsmen   73
   Chapter X: The Bishops' Estates   79
   Chapter XI: Church Building   84

Part Four: The World Beyond the Diocese
   Chapter XII: The Bishops and the Nation   92
   Chapter XIII: Bishops and Popes   108

Afterword   114

Appendices:
   i   Names of Members of Religious Communities   115
   ii Charities at Home and Abroad   116
   iii Oratories and Chapels   119

Index   134

REFERENCES

This book is a guide to the Bishops' Registers 1264–1559 as they have been presented by a succession of editors and published by the Somerset Record Society between 1887 and 2021. The following bibliography explains the references to them used throughout the text:

Droxford: *Calendar of the Register of John de Drokensford, Bishop of Bath and Wells (A.D. 1309–1329)*, edited by Right Rev. Bishop Hobhouse (Somerset Record Society i. 1887)

Ralph: *The Register of Ralph of Shrewsbury, Bishop of Bath and Wells 1329–1363*, edited by Thomas Scott Holmes, M.A. (Somerset Record Society ix and x, 1896)

Giffard & Bowett: *The Registers of Walter Giffard, Bishop of Bath and Wells, 1265–6, and of Henry Bowett, Bishop of Bath and Wells, 1401–7*, edited by Thomas Scott Holmes, M.A. (Somerset Record Society xiii, 1899)

Bubwith: *The Register of Nicholas Bubwith, Bishop of Bath and Wells, 1407–1424*, edited by Thomas Scott Holmes, D.D. (Somerset Record Society xxix and xxx, 1914)

Stafford: *The Register of John Stafford, Bishop of Bath and Wells, 1425–1443*, edited by Thomas Scott Holmes, D.D. (Somerset Record Society xxxi and xxxii, 1915–16)

Bekynton: *The Register of Thomas Bekynton, Bishop of Bath and Wells, 1443–1465*, edited by Sir H.C. Maxwell-Lyte, K.C.B. and M.C.B. Dawes, F.S.A. (Somerset Record Society xlix and l (1934–5)

Stillington & Fox: *The Registers of Robert Stillington, Bishop of Bath and Wells 1466–1491, and Richard Fox, Bishop of Bath and Wells 1492–1494*, edited by Sir H.C. Maxwell-Lyte, K.C.B. (Somerset Record Society lii, 1937)

King & Hadrian: *The Registers of Oliver King, Bishop of Bath and Wells 1496–1503, and Hadrian de Castello, Bishop of Bath and Wells 1503–1518*, edited by Sir Henry Maxwell-Lyte, K.C.B. (Somerset Record Society liv, 1939)

Wolsey, etc: *The Registers of Thomas Wolsey, Bishop of Bath and Wells 1518–1523, John Clerke, Bishop of Bath and Wells 1523–1541, William Knyght, Bishop of Bath and Wells 1541–1547, and Gilbert Bourne, Bishop of Bath and Wells 1554–1559*, edited by Sir Henry Maxwell-Lyte, K.C.B. (Somerset Record Society lv, 1940)

Oridination Lists: *Bath & Wells Ordinations, 1564–1526*, ed. R.W. Dunning (Somerset Record Society xcix, 2021)

The other abbreviations are:
S.H.C.   Somerset Heritage Centre
S.R.S.   Somerset Record Society

LIST OF ILLUSTRATIONS

1. The dramatic opening of Bishop Stillington's register, 1466: S.H.C. D/D/B reg 7, f. 8b — 10
2. 'Institution to the same church inserted in a sheet annexed at the following sign': S.H.C. D/D/B reg 4, f. 3d — 11
3. The work of a bored registry clerk in the 17th century: S.H.C. D/D/B reg 4, f. 102d — 12
4. John Storthwayt, registrar, uses his initials as cross-references in Bishop Bowet's register, 1406: S.H.C. D/D/B reg 3, fos. 39, 41 — 14
5. William Bowerman, registrar and notary, signs off the ordination list for 22 March 1516: S.H.C. D/D/B reg 10, f. 158b — 15
6. John Storthwayt notes fees paid [6d and 12d] and other fees unpaid ['because he was a clerk of the Reverend Father Nicholas Bubwyth'], 1408: S.H.C. D/D/B reg 3, f. 47 — 15
7. John Storthwayt notes unpaid fees for business done by the vicar-general, Richard Pittes, in Salisbury, 1406: S.H.C. D/D/B reg 3, ff. 41–2 — 16
8. Memorial brass to Thomas Golde, esquire, 1525, Crewkerne church: reproduced from A.B. Connor, *Monumental Brasses in Somerset* (Kingsmead Reprints, Bath, 1970), plate LXI — 25
9. The chapel in the right wing of Blackmoor Farm, Cannington, 1859: engraving by A.A. Clarke — 44
10. The new village church of Farleigh Hungerford, replacing the original that became the castle chapel in 1443: photograph, Author — 87
11. The 'rebus' or badge of Bishop Thomas Bekynton – a beacon and a barrel (tun) above a letter T, Bishop's Eye, Wells: reproduced from H.E. Reynolds, *Wells Cathedral: its Foundation, Constitutional History and Statutes* (1881) — 90
12. Master David Price becomes vicar-general when Bishop Stafford goes to France with the royal household in March 1430: S.H.C. D/D/B reg 5, f. 56 — 101
13. Bishop Stafford resumes business on his return from France in September 1430: S.H.C. D/D/B reg 5, f. 57 — 101
14. John Roland begins his duties as vicar-general when Bishop Bubwith attends the Council of Constance, 1414: S.H.C. D/D/B reg 4, f. 88. The later registry clerk is at work again. — 112
15. Hymerford House, East Coker: reproduced from *Batten's South Somerset Villages* by John Batten, F.S.A. (Somerset Books, 1994), opp. p. 169 — 126

ACKNOWLEDGEMENTS

I want to pay tribute to the scholars who made the Bath and Wells Bishops' Registers publicly available through the medium of the Somerset Record Society and its faithful subscribers – Bishop Edmund Hobhouse, the Revd James Bennett, the Revd (later Canon) T. Scott Holmes, Sir Henry Maxwell-Lyte and Mr. M.C. B Dawes; and to a succession of Diocesan Registrars who first compiled and guarded, and later permitted study of those Registers. And I offer thanks to Dr Andrew Butcher, Professor Ralph Griffiths, Mr William Hancock, Professor Michael Hicks and Dr Adrian Webb who have given this Guide their support. Dr Webb took the photographs from the registers and designed the book's cover.

The publication of illustrations from the original registers is with the permission of Somerset Archives and Local Studies.

INTRODUCTION

The volumes of the Somerset Record Society, now almost one hundred in number, can present a formidable challenge. The titles on their spines, many in Latin, often hide their contents. It is the object of this and perhaps further additional volumes, supplementary to the Society's main series, to make such titles more user-friendly by showing that what seems to be exclusively for the specialist historian is information of much wider interest. Sometimes, unfortunately, the indexes also seem to hide more than they reveal. This volume about bishops' registers is not simply a general study of how bishops operated in Somerset at a time when most of our characteristic church towers were built. It also draws attention to the many aspects of local life and family connection that became the bishops' concern and which are still of interest today.

The diocese of Bath & Wells almost exactly fitted the county of Somerset until boundary changes in the 19th century, and so the records of the bishops involved people and events stretching from the river Avon in what is now very near the centre of Bristol, south to the Dorset border between Yeovil and Sherborne (in Salisbury diocese), the Devon border just beyond Chard (Exeter diocese), and Devon and Exeter again on the heights of Exmoor. Its coast from beyond Minehead up to the Severn estuary looked across to Wales, to the diocese of St David's in the west and, as the Channel narrowed, to Llandaff. Most of Bristol and its northern hinterland were in Worcester diocese.

Bishops at the time were powerful men. They were appointed by kings (and approved by popes), they were seen by both as their agents and supporters, and they had often been (some still were) senior civil servants and government ministers. They often knew kings personally, were members of the upper house of Parliament as well as the Church's own assembly known as Convocation, and were thus involved both in levying and collecting (as well, of course, as paying) taxes. Pages of their registers concerned paying, or not paying, what the Pope or the King demanded. More entries concerned the Law: the law of the land involving property rights (the right to appoint a parish priest in particular), and peaceable behaviour; and the law of the Church, known as Canon Law, which claimed the right to try clergymen, and to deal with moral offences. In the earliest surviving church court at Wells covering the last forty years of the 15th century a quarter of the cases were marriage disputes, over a fifth were classed as perjury (including debt, which was seen as a breach of contract), a fifth were defamation or slander, and others of failing to pay agreed sums to clergymen or of failing to carry out the terms of a will.[1]

The bishop was also, for the time he was bishop, as big a landowner as most in Somerset, with a palace at Wells and large houses across the county, a house in Hampshire, conveniently on the road to London, and another in the capital. Documents relating to estates attached to those houses are often found in the registers and offer glimpses of farming activities and the problems that most other landowners faced.

So, the bishop was a hugely influential figure in Somerset society, touching people, whether they liked it or not. Occasional documents in the registers show small groups of knights, squires and clerks of the bishop's chapel witnessing formal business, and 'valets' and other servants who kept the bishop's show on the road, almost constantly on the move around the diocese and to

---

[1] R.W. Dunning, 'The Wells Consistory Court in the Fifteenth Century' in *Proceedings of the Somersetshire Archaeological and Natural History Society*, 106 (1962), 46–61.

London or wherever Parliament and Convocation met. Among Bishop Droxford's household were Adam 'le chapeman', who bought provisions, William le Yonge 'of our Butlery', in charge of wine and beer, Robert of Somerton, who served in the bishop's wardrobe, Nicholas de Camme, valet of his chamber, Alan Pomeroy, clerk of his household, Walter of Wherwell, his barber, and Alan his messenger. And all these men, together with legal advisers and a doctor, wore the bishop's livery according to their personal status. Nicholas de Bath, one of the bishop's lawyers, had a small annual retainer of 26s 8d, a third of a length of cloth 'as worn by the bishop's clerks', and lambswool linings for his surcoat and hood (Droxford pp. 76, 121–2, 134, 142,156, 174, 222, 239, 265).

Bishop Ralph's register does not show much sign of such opulence, but the bishop was surrounded by servants when he and they were kidnapped for a night in Yeovil in 1349 by an armed gang (Ralph nos. 2301, 2303). More than ten years earlier the same bishop's progress in the south of the diocese involved on one day as many as fifty-five horsemen.[1] The ageing Bishop Ralph Erghum remembered in his will in 1398 what sounds a rather more modest entourage: a chaplain cross-bearer, a 'palfreman' (groom), two 'cherieters', and valets, pages, clerks and chapel boys.[2]

The registers also contain information on much more public affairs: examples of what would now be called crowd-funding for all kinds of local, national and even international good causes for communities and individuals; settlements of local disputes and traces of national, and even international, ones; attempts to raise the standards of behaviour in abbeys and priories; punishments for unseemly behaviour; righting a huge variety of wrongs against oppressed individuals – information on the good and the bad of Somerset and beyond for two centuries and more.

---

[1] 'Household Roll of Bishop Ralph of Shrewsbury' in *Collectanea I*, ed. T.F. Palmer (S.R.S. xxxix, 1924), 72–174.
[2] *Somerset Medieval Wills, 1501–1530*, ed. F.W. Weaver (S.R.S. xix, 1903), 294–7.

And, among a mass of technical information, formally set down, there are wonderful glimpses of very human behaviour of the bishops themselves, faithfully recorded (whatever might have been his motives) by an assiduous or mischievous clerk in the bishop's secretariat. Bishop Droxford ordered his principal law officer (Official Principal, usually simply Official) not to take action against the rector of Tintinhull, whose name he (a rather embarrassed bishop) did not know (Droxford p. 43). Bishop Ralph, no doubt very annoyed by being embroiled in a lawsuit, ordered his household staff not to open the door to a legal messenger who came overnight from Wells to Wiveliscombe to serve a writ on him. The frustrated messenger evidently committed the whole affair to writing, and the bishop's clerk, evidently feeling some sympathy for the poor man, saw fit to record the whole affair (Ralph no. 2466). When Sir William Bonville presented John Keche as the next rector of Sock Dennis in 1434, Bishop Stafford remembered he had appointed a rector only five years earlier (Stafford nos. 216, 463). Bishop Bekynton's registry clerk, recording the appointment of a new vicar of Locking in 1445, dated the event 'at Bagshot ... at the inn marked with the sign of the Crown, at which the bishop was wont to lodge when travelling there.' The same bishop, making his protege, Andrew Holes, archdeacon of Wells in 1449 without telling him 'appeared to be not well pleased' when Holes asked for time to consider (Bekynton nos. 138, 474, 503, 507). The bishops were human and their registrars were determined to record their personal characteristics.

PART ONE: THE REGISTERS

CHAPTER I
HOW THE REGISTERS WERE MADE

Bishops' registers survive as bound volumes (earlier ones from Lincoln, York and Exeter were rolls), written on parchment, compiled, mostly in Latin, by clerks either as continuing day-to-day records or from files or other original material. They were essential at the time as legal precedents recording appointments to parishes and cathedral posts and as records of the creation of clergymen.

The Bishops' Archives
Bishop Droxford declared in 1311 that he was embarrassed that his predecessors' registers had still not been handed over to him two years after his election, but at the end of that year, when the Dynham family's right to present a rector to Corton Denham was challenged, he was able to discover that over forty years before Oliver de Dynham had presented Henry de Montford (Droxford pp. 38, 55). Bishop Bubwith in 1410 appointed three cathedral canons and the vicar of St Cuthbert's, Wells, to denounce 'certain sons of iniquity' who had stolen the diocesan archives – 'charters, instruments, books, compositions, *judicia* (judgments), *arbitria* (decisions) and other muniments, both spiritual and temporal', presumably including registers – and to see that they were returned (Bubwith no. 238). In 1443 the archbishop of Canterbury ordered 'all letters, evidences, muniments, registers and seals' to be handed over immediately to the new bishop, Bekynton (Bekynton no. 1), and Bishop Bekynton's register

covering the next twenty years shows how useful they were. Thus in 1464 when, in reply to a demand from the Exchequer court for information about the church of Marston Magna, the bishop (or more likely his registrar), after searching 'the registers and other evidences' was able to trace the first vicar there back to the reign of Henry III and to prove that the nuns of Polsloe priory, near Exeter, had been rectors since 1197–8 (Bekynton no. 1541).[1] The records, in one form or another, thus reached back into the 12th century, and such information often cannot be found elsewhere.

There were, it becomes clear, writings in the bishop's custody, in the immediate care of his registrar, from the time before registers in this diocese are known to have existed.[2] There were also court and account rolls of the bishops' estates that were essential for all stewards and receivers to be sure that each bishop received the income that was his due so that he could maintain his household and dispense proper hospitality. On occasion, records of Wells cathedral (Droxford p. 24; Ralph nos. 1203, 2480; Bubwith no. 136; King & Hadrian no. 470), Bath cathedral priory (known known as abbey) (Bekynton no. 296), St John's hospital, Bath (Bekynton no. 1642) and Athelney abbey (King & Hadrian no. 956) were consulted to answer particular questions and, when necessary, they were copied into registers. Even the archives of an individual parish priest, remarkably preserved, once proved so vital that copies were made. Those involved the income of the vicar of Pilton and included a writing of Bishop Jocelin of 1233, recited and confirmed by Bishop Ralph in 1349, recited and confirmed by Bishop Harewell in 1377, all three compared with the originals, entered into the register and signed by the registrar, Robert Williamson. They are followed in the register with a certificate that on a particular day in 1504, in the cloister of Wells cathedral before witnesses, a notary had seen, handled

---

[1] The assiduous John Collinson had noted that entry in Bekynton's register: *The History and Antiquities of the County of Somerset* (Bath, 1791), ii. 374.
[2] Hugh, bishop of Lincoln 1209–35 (brother of Jocelin of Wells) was the first bishop known to have recorded his business in rolls (rather than in books), and rolls were used at York and Exeter.

and examined the originals produced by the vicar and also the transcripts in the register (King & Hadrian nos. 569–72).

Records of the actions of the bishops themselves dated back to the time of Bishop Savaric (1192–1205) and were copied in later registers as required, their originals either ready to hand or willingly lent by their owners. Most were from the long reign of Bishop Jocelin (1206–42), but there were others from their successors: William of Bitton I (1248–64), William of Bitton II (1267–74), Robert Burnell (1275–92), William of March (1293–1302), and Walter Haselshaw (1302–8). Meanwhile there is a register covering most of the short stay of Bishop Walter Giffard in the diocese, 1265–6. It is so short there is very little to discover about how Giffard ruled, but after a note that a new rector had been presented to Pendomer, his clerk wrote 'cancelled because registered elsewhere' (Giffard & Bowett no. xli). From this note it can be assumed that there was a second form of record that has been lost. What survives from Giffard's time are two quires of parchment, folded so as to record business from the archdeaconry of Wells, the jurisdictions (areas of government) of the dean of Wells and the abbot of Glastonbury together, and from the archdeaconries of Taunton and Bath in turn. The registry clerks took the incomplete sheets to York where Giffard had been appointed archbishop, and continued to fill them up with York business.[1] They were eventually bound together in a single volume and still remain at York. One separate piece of Bath & Wells business also went to York and was later stitched to the edge of a sheet in the correct chronological order (Giffard & Bowett pp. 7–8).

The register of John Droxford or Drokensford (bishop 1309–29), the next to survive, covers most of the years of his episcopate. He or his registrar evidently intended business to be arranged in separate categories – royal letters, estate and household business, institutions and inductions (that is appointments) of clergy, dispensations (relaxing of Church regulations) and licences to study (and thus be absent from parishes), public letters, copies

---

[1] See David M. Smith, *Guide to Bishops' Registers of England and Wales* (Royal Historical Society, 1981), 31, 234.

of special correspondence – but, as a commentator remarks, 'unfortunately these divisions are by no means adhered to all the time'.[1] The register as it survives is disorganised, starting with business of 1332–3, immediately followed by more for 1315–16, with the real beginning of general business on folio 27 and gatherings for royal writs starting at folio 43a (p. 55) and public letters on folio 51 (Droxford pp. 26, 58). Droxford certainly kept a separate record of ordinations above the rank of *tonsurati*,[2] for a search in 1336 discovered that Mr John de Faryngdon was made acolyte on 24 September 1317, just after being made rector of North Barrow, and he was subsequently made sub-deacon (Ralph, nos. 17, 167, 1073). Otherwise, the tonsure ceremonies were noted almost informally wherever they took place, Baldwin Mohun, for instance, in the bishop's chapel at Kingsbury Episcopi at the beginning of November 1315 (Droxford p. 100)

The register of Bishop Ralph of Shrewsbury (bishop 1329–63) is mostly arranged as a single chronological record, though two sections of royal letters, now bound between gatherings, suggest that they were collected and recorded separately. Some memoranda seem to have been entered where space permitted, one requesting a search for a 1350 ordination ordered by the bishop's Official, Thomas Buckton, and two others involving judgements by him. No register of ordinations has survived, though the bishop, apparently himself, searched the register in 1353 for the name of Richard atte Wode or Compton, made sub-deacon at Wiveliscombe on 20 December 1349, deacon at Bath cathedral priory on 18 September 1350, and priest on 12 March 1351 at Wiveliscombe (Ralph nos. 2396–8, 2756). Bishop Ralph's register is incomplete, covering only the years 1329–54 in the volume that bears his name, and a fragment for 1362–3 is bound up with Droxford's register (but printed at the end of Ralph's printed register).

---

[1] Ibid. 31.
[2] Men having the first tonsure, the first of the principal clerical orders, followed by acolyte, sub-deacon, deacon and priest.

There is a gap in the surviving registers until 1401 and then an almost complete series[1] until 1554. When the registers of John Barnet (1363–6), John Harewell (1367–86), Walter Skirlaw 1386–8) and Ralph Erghum (1388–1400) were lost is not known, though Bishop Bubwith was asked to search all records back to 1377 for details of appointments to Norton sub Hamdon. If he did so successfully, there is no record. Bubwith's register also contains reference to a testimonial letter, sealed by Bishop Harewell, which may have been a copy of the entry in Bishop Ralph's register dated 31 December 1362, sealed by Bishop Harewell, appointing a prior of Burtle (Ralph, no. *110, Bubwith nos. 183, 1149).

Bishop Bowet's register is a general record of acts arranged in chronological order and finishing with acts of his successor, Bishop Bubwith. Those are largely repeated in Bubwith's own register which, however, begins in some disarray and starts again, from 1408, on p. 22 of the printed edition. It is thereafter a general, chronological record, followed by a separately-kept register of elections to heads of religious houses and another of ordinations, usually from acolytes to priests. Bubwith's successors, John Stafford (1425–43), Thomas Bekynton (1443–65), Robert Stillington (1466–91) and the rest followed that pattern, though the printed editions of registers after Bekynton's omit the registers of ordinations. There is no record of ordinations after 1526 until 1554. Ordination lists 1465–1526 have now been gathered in a single printed volume published by the Somerset Record Society in 2021. One singular feature of the register of Bishop Stillington is the elaborate initial on the title page featuring a fashionably-dressed cross-bowman, perhaps heralding a new leader for a new age.

---

[1] Longleat House MS. 5105 contains two extracts, one from Bishop Clerke's register (Wolsey, etc, no. 169), the other from Bishop Barlow's missing register, probably made about 1558 when Sir John Thynne presented a new rector to Chedzoy: D.M. Smith, *Supplement to the Guide to Bishops' Registers of England and Wales*, Canterbury & York Society, 2004), 7; Wolsey, etc, no. 900.

1 *The dramatic opening of Bishop Stillington's register, 1466: S.H.C. D/D/B reg 7, f. 8b*

The registers contain a few clues about how they were actually made. The 'registry' seems, in the time of Bishop Droxford, to have been simply the place where papers that the bishop's registrar carried with him were kept: in 1315 they were 'in the chapel in the court house at Wiveliscombe next to the bishop's chamber'. In the 1320s important documents were kept in the Treasury in Wells cathedral (Droxford pp. 91, 180, 186, 270). Bishop Bubwith's registry in 1415 was in St John's hospital, Wells, but Bekynton's registrar had an office in the bishop's house in London and another somewhere in Wells (Bubwith no. 556; Bekynton nos. 172, 1179).

The Registry and the Registrars
A bishop's registry was not only a place but a busy organisation, to judge by the number of documents that still survive as copies in the registers. Exactly how each office was organised we cannot know, though it was headed by a registrar and probably included several 'chapel' or 'writing' clerks. One such clerk, involved in copying some of Bubwith's early acts from Bowet's register, used a sign [8z] to note the completion of the business in question and to refer to a *cedula* (a sheet) recording it.

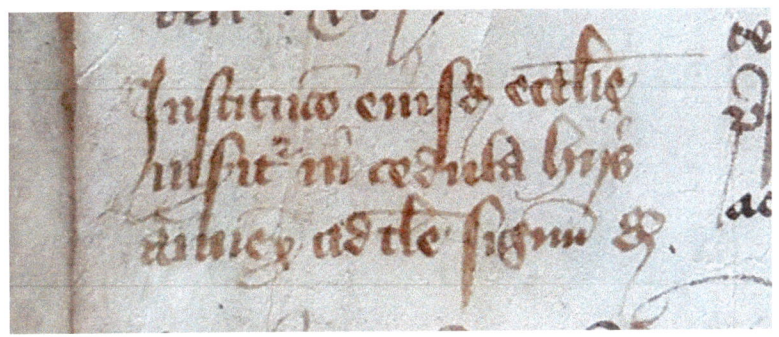

2 'Institution to the same church inserted in a sheet annexed at the following sign': S.H.C.D/D/B reg 4, f. 3d.

The same word was used when a clergyman resigned his office, in that case a sheet of parchment which he held in his hand before the bishop, the contents of which were duly copied in the register (Bubwith nos. 36, 70). The resignation of the rector of Kittisford, sealed with the seal of the archdeacon of Taunton, was in 1314 'deposited in *phylacio* (a file) in duplicate' (Droxford, p. 164), and twice in Bekynton's time documents of a temporary nature were mentioned. One 'hangs among the lord's files (*philarcia*) for the year 1458' and the other 'on the file (*filarcio*) for this year' [1460] (Bekynton nos. 1179, 1305, from S.H.C. D/D/B reg 6, ff. 132, 156).[1] A registry clerk of a much later date used a space in Bubwith's register to indulge a flight of fancy, or perhaps to vent his feelings against his superior.

3   *The work of a bored registry clerk in the 17th century: S.H.C. D/D/B reg 4, f. 102d.*

A registrar is mentioned three times in Droxford's register as keeper of documents, but is never named (Droxford pp. 79,

---

[1] The system was used in Worcester diocese in the 1380s: *A Calendar of the Register of Henry Wakefield, Bishop of Worcester 1375–95*, ed. W.P. Marett (The Worcestershire Historical Society, 1972), no. 206.

215–16). Robert Chigwell or Chilkwell[1] in 1330 and William de Ludeford[2] in 1335 were registrars in Bishop Ralph's time, and Roger de Tybryghton in 1353 copied out a long papal letter (Ralph nos. 222, 949, 2737). Later registrars were named and clearly had become valued members of each bishop's administration. John Storthwayt, registrar of Bishop Bowet, was also the bishop's *barbitonsor*, shaving each man's head as he came for his first tonsure (Giffard & Bowett nos. 236, 307). Storthwayt's initials and name also appear in the margins of the register that the editor ignored!

Storthwayt went on to higher office under bishops Bubwith and Stafford and was also employed as a royal commissioner and diplomat.[3] Robert Williamson,[4] appointed by Bishop Fox to be registrar of his chancery (secretariat) and audience (court) in 1493, left his mark prominently in the registers of bishops Fox, King and Hadrian until 1513 (Stillington & Fox no. 1174; King & Hadrian nos. 62, 100, 249, 571, 930, 942, 1039). William Bowerman, Williamson's eventual successor, took over writing the ordination lists in April 1514, was appointed registrar just over a year later (King & Hadrian no. 1153) and subscribed his name to the lists of March 1516 and March 1518 (Ordination lists, nos. 220–1).

Patrick White, Bowerman's successor, seems to have been less assiduous, preferring several times in 1525–6 to 'note' documents rather than copying them out in full (Wolsey, etc. nos. 240–1, 245, 247, 249, 254, 256, 470).

Clergy paid fees to the registrar to record their ordinations and other appointments, and in 1318 John Walwayn was awarded a

---

[1] He was subsequently in the service of Queen Philippa and later in the royal chancery, and was often Ralph of Shrewsbury's proxy in Parliament: *Proctors for Parliament: Clergy, Community and Politics c. 1248–1539*, ed. P. Bradford and A.K. McHardy, i (Canterbury and York Society 107, 2017), 113, 127, 134, 145, 148, 168, 237.

[2] Later rector of Kilmington: Ralph, nos. 1391, 1405, 1831.

[3] A.B. Emden, *Biographical Register of the University of Oxford to 1500* (Oxford, 1957–9), iii. 1792–3.

[4] A.B. Emden, *Biographical Register of the University of Cambridge to 1500* (Cambridge, 1963), 640–1.

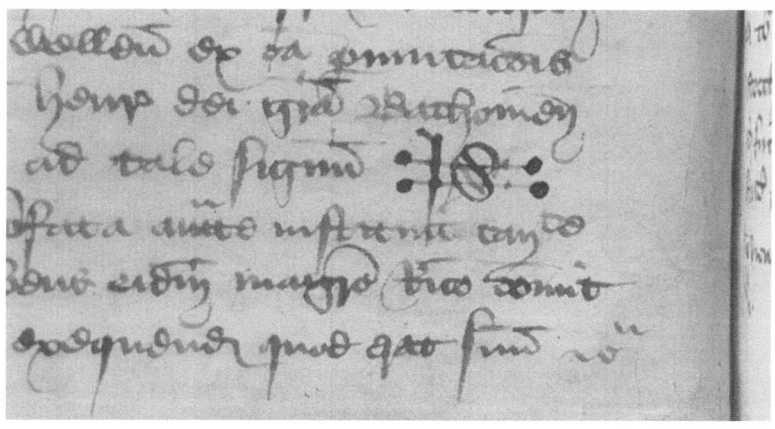

4 John Storthwayt, registrar, uses his initials as cross-references in Bishop Bowet's register, 1406: S.H.C. D/D/B reg 3, fos. 39, 41.

small pension from these accumulated funds until a benefice could be found for him (Droxford, p. 12). John Storthwayt added notes into the margins of Bishop Bowet's register when fees were either not paid or waived (the editor noted some of them) and when he had paid them over to the bishop.

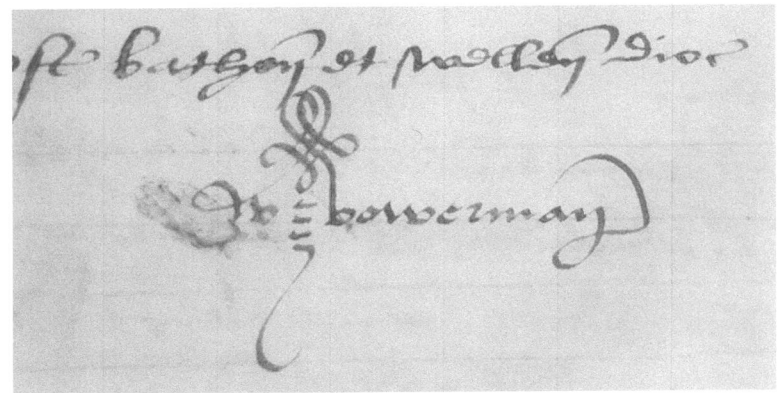

5   William Bowerman, registrar and notary, signs off the ordination list for 22 March 1516: S.H.C. D/D/B reg 10, f. 158b.

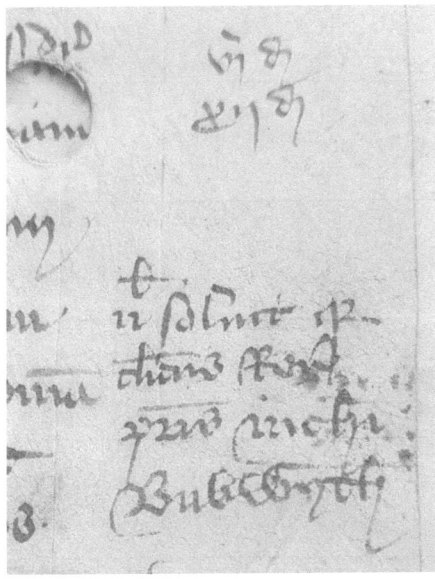

6   John Storthwayt notes fees paid [6d and 12d] and other fees unpaid ['because he was a clerk of the Reverend Father Nicholas Bubwyth'], 1408: S.H.C. D/D/B reg 3, f. 47

Storthwayt also noted the loss of his fees when the vicar-general did business without him at his house in Salisbury (Giffard & Bowett, nos. 178, 186, 189, 236, 307, 315).

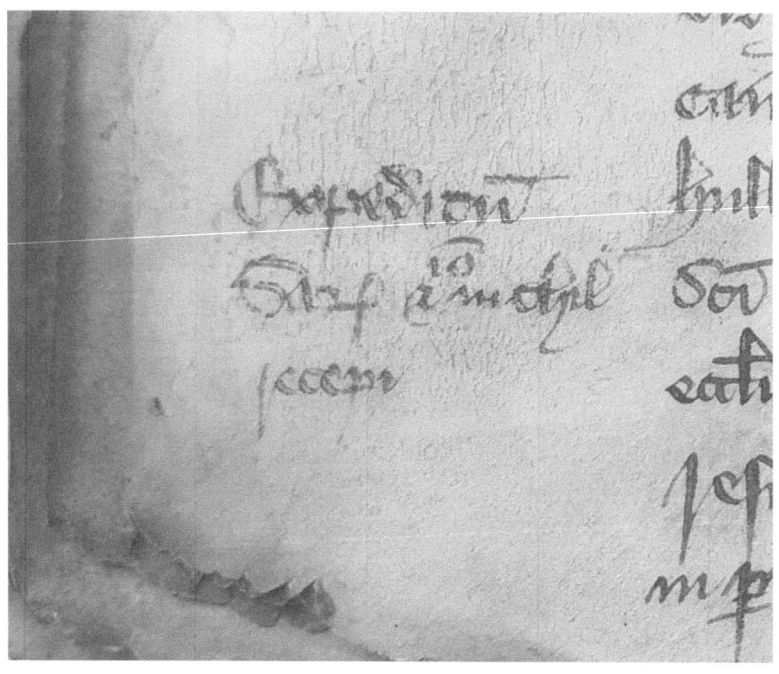

7   *John Storthwayt notes unpaid fees for business done by the vicar-general, Richard Pittes, while in Salisbury, 1406 ['Business done at Salisbury, therefore I have received nothing']: S.H.C. D/D/B reg 3, f. 41*

To authenticate all formal documents bishops, like others in authority, needed a seal. Bishop Droxford, so his register tells us, had two, a larger, formal, one, often called a 'great' seal, a 'small' or business seal, and a 'privy' one (Droxford, pp. 48, 55). Bishop Ralph used his 'privy' seal for personal correspondence (Ralph, no. 2807). Bishop Bubwith, translated from the diocese of London in something of a hurry, had to use his old London 'great' seal for his first documents before a new one could be made (Bubwith, nos. 78, 708, 716). Both Bishop Clerke in 1523 and Bishop Bourne in 1554 also needed time for a seal to be produced, and both used the seals of the bishops of London until they had their own (Wolsey, etc. nos. 143, 664).

PART TWO:
THE PEOPLE IN THE REGISTERS

CHAPTER II
LAY PEOPLE AND THE BISHOP

The indexes to the printed registers contain the names of thousands of people, the essential materials for family history. Many of them were clergy who were probably not all Somerset natives and who were not expected to have offspring, but all were members of families, building blocks in the construction of genealogies. Rather fewer named in the registers were lay people, usually local landowners appearing as patrons of livings, prosperous people who were friends of bishops. Fewer were substantial parishioners whose support or opinions were required, a few were devout folk who wanted to go on pilgrimage, become recluses or hermits (see Chapter V) or otherwise show their practical support for their parish churches. And even fewer were serfs, unfree labourers on the bishops' manors, whose promising sons were first made free (manumitted) and then tonsured, their futures usually already mapped out as junior clergy to be employed only within the diocese as clerical assistants in parishes. And there were those who found themselves in trouble for misbehaviour of many kinds. Together they were the ancestors, direct or indirect, of those whose names begin to appear more regularly in the parish registers of the 16th century.

The Beginnings of Traceable Families

In a period when inherited family names were beginning to emerge, the tiny word 'de' often signified the owner of property – Sir John de Clyvedon was, clearly enough, the lord of the manor of Clevedon. By contrast, the 'de' in the name of John de Hountenpath of West Buckland, a serf on the bishops' manor there freed in 1326, meant that he lived by the hunting path that ran through the parish, just as John attemore of Wellington, freed in 1322, and John attenaysh of the bishops' manor of Pucklechurch in Gloucestershire were known by the moor and the ash tree where they lived. John Sibley, a serf of Kingsbury Episcopi, already had a name still to be found within a few miles of the village (Droxford, pp. 189, 197, 254, 259). Other surname origins are to be found in the group of leading parishioners of Henstridge that came together to act as guarantors when Bishop Ralph consecrated their newly-built church in 1332. The registrar described them as a jury – twelve men sworn to stand by the bishop should anyone dispute his action. Two of them had occupational names, Le Warynner (keeper of the rabbit or hare warren) and Le Smyth; three were named from the hamlets where they lived, Thomere, Thornezete, Merssch; one was 'Le Heir'. Of the rest there were two Bassets, a Symond and a Phelip, names still recognisable today (Ralph, no. 410). Nine of those twelve, as might be expected, were familiar and established men, among the tax payers of the large village community in 1327.[1]

Twenty years later a piece of business involving the bishop's estate recorded the names of some of his tenants and those of a county jury. The tenants, eight residents of Dulcote and one of Easton, both just outside Wells, included three with occupation names – John le Carpunter, Robert le Marlere, William Frankelyn and John Butiler; two with places of origin – Dulcote and Wellesleigh; and Geoffrey Burgeis, perhaps reflecting his or a forebear's status in Wells. The jury of eleven, summoned by Thomas Cary of Kingsdon as escheator to declare that a grant of land would not harm the king's interests, had names pointing to Draycott, Martock, Combe Hay, Cockhill

---

[1] *Kirby's Quest for Somerset ...*, ed. F.H. Dickinson (S.R.S. iii, 1889), 218–19.

and Ashwick and the patronymics Fykeys, Bithewell, Wynd, Chestre and Bewel (Ralph, no. 2681).

By the later years of the 15th century other groups of laymen emerged. Bishops had to be careful that patrons presenting clergy to them for appointment to parishes had the right to do so, and from the 1480s a local 'jury' of twelve, half laymen and half clergy, made enquiries when necessary. So, in April 1445 an enquiry was held in Brushford church as to who was the legal patron of the living. Thomas Copleston of Luccombe, William Clowesham and William Allercote of Timberscombe, John Stowye of Cutcombe, Patrick Forster of Wootton Courtenay, Richard Stucle of Minehead and John Curre of Brushford and eight local clergymen decided in favour of the sisters Joan Crosse, widow, Agnes Riphay and Thomasia Lawher – together they were ten members of established West Somerset families (Bekynton, no. 135). Similar later enquiries produced the names of more leading lay people.

In 1483 the rectory of Norton Fitzwarren became vacant and Robert Kooper of Norton, and James Newham, Walter Eston, William Bedell, Ralph Buclande and Thomas Bonde, all of Taunton, were summoned with six neighbouring clergy (Stillington & Fox, no. 694). The vacancy at Shepton Mallet in 1488 involved eight laymen, seven from Shepton and Philip Bisse of Stoke St Michael (Stillington & Fox, no. 909). Philip Bisse's name appears as one of the first generation of the Bysse family, known from his will dated 1519.[1] He was thus already regarded as a man of substance and fount of local knowledge nearly a quarter century earlier. Similar groups were consulted about North Cadbury and Sandford Orcas in 1490, Castle Cary in 1492, Uphill, St Mary's, Taunton, Charlton Musgrove and Exton in 1497, Saltford and Hornblotton in 1505. A much larger group than usual was summoned for the vacancy at Winford in 1499 because the matter was in dispute between three men of influence, Sir John Rodney, Humphrey Baskerwyle and Edmund Basset. Fifteen clergy and thirteen laymen as well as the claimants were summoned to Wells, seven clergy and seven laymen (including

---

[1] *Somerset and Dorset Notes and Queries*, xxxix, 51.

one each not so summoned) actually turned up, and a vicar was duly appointed (Stillington & Fox, nos. 968–9, 1018, King & Hadrian, nos. 40–3, 161–2, 200–1, 651, 658, 660). Thirty leaders of the community between Wells and Bristol.

More men, and the places where they lived, can be discovered among the acolytes, and sometimes among the sub-deacons, in the ordinations lists from 1445 (Bekynton, no. 1662) until the 1480s and resumed 1518–22 (Ordination Lists). Many acolytes proceeded no further in the clerical life, using the grade to further their education, perhaps becoming writing clerks, schoolmasters or even lawyers. Among them were William Powncett of Castle Cary, made acolyte in 1518, and William Collard of Wiveliscombe in 1522, who do not appear as beneficed clergy later, but who may have followed secular paths; both were members of families present in those places four centuries later.

Groups of names could also be found when members of monastic communities were sometimes listed. So, when Willelma de Blachyngdon, prioress of Cannington, died in 1336, the remaining thirteen nuns were named in the register to record the election of her successor. Seven of them had names showing their place of birth or family origin, mostly in Somerset; five, in spite of eccentric spelling, seem to have belonged to recognisable West Country families (Ralph, no. 1332). The canons of Taunton, also present at an election three years later, appear to have been of more scattered origins. The new prior, Robert de Messingham, seems from his name to have come from north Lincolnshire; John Godalming and Robert de Alresford hailed from the diocese of Winchester (the bishop was patron of the priory) and Ralph de Colmpstoke (Culmstock), the retiring prior, from Devon. Most of the rest bore Somerset village names, but two, Roger Samuel and John Isaac, had obviously different origins (Ralph, no. 1332). The Taunton community in 1413 all bore family surnames, some deriving from place-names and most still current (Bubwith, no. 1272). Appendix I contains references in the registers to lists of community members recorded at visitations and elections.

The register of Bishop Bekynton the last detailed one of the diocese, provides a glimpse of a bishop dealing with laymen as well as with clergy. In the first two years of his rule, he permitted the elderly Martin Jacob and his wife Joan, of North Petherton, to have services in their own house because travel to their parish church had become difficult; he allowed Stephen Coye to become a hermit; he brought the full power of church law against William Tylly of Midsomer Norton, John Uphill and John Baker the younger of Bedminster, John Rew of Wells and his former servant Joan Spere, Roger Norys of Bishop's Hull and his servant Katherine, John Rewe for adultery, the others for offences unspecified. He appointed Edward Hulle, esquire, and William Bery as temporary guardians of the lands of Stogursey priory and Hugh Kene of Martock similarly at Stoke sub Hamdon college; and John Gayton as surveyor of his own estates. And in those two years he recruited a regular household of whom most were laymen – Anthony Vilate, his chief messenger, John Gauter the younger, his accountant and bailiff, Thomas Dodyng, his butler (clerk of his kitchen), John Lambyn, another accountant, John Gauter the elder, John Happesford, esquire, Richard Erle and John Germayn (Bekynton, nos. 17, 32, 36, 38–9, 41, 62, 68, 70, 92, 121, 123, 139, 179). Robert Stowell, esquire, was one of three witnesses to the bishop's will.[1] Most of these names will be welcome additions to family histories.

Two Somerset Families: the Montagues and the Goldes
A survey of appointments of rectors to just a few parishes recorded in the registers may well bring to light information that creates or improves the family trees of those who made them. The senior Montagues were well-known beyond Somerset and their actions as patrons of Chedzoy, Donyatt and Yarlington show them playing their considerable part in the community. Their junior relatives were involved with Sutton Montis and Weston Bampfylde. The Goldes, less significant still, were responsible only for Seaborough.

The Montagues could trace their origins without difficulty back to the 12th century and their name to the steep-sided hill adjoining Ham Hill that gave its name to the village below.

---
[1] *Somerset Medieval Wills (1383–1500)*, ed. F.W. Weaver (S.R.S. xvi, 1901), 207.

Their first distinguished ancestor was William who in 1255 was brought by Bishop William Bitton I to agree terms with the rector of his home parish of Donyatt about the chapel he had built and how it might have services without damage to the parish church (Droxford, pp. 152–3).

Simon, William's heir, probably fought in Wales in 1277[1] but first appears in Droxford's register in 1311 because, a year earlier, he had vowed to visit the Holy Land before Midsummer and had not done so. The reason why was that he was in prison, probably for an offence against Forest Law.[2] Breaking his solemn vow was a bigger offence and he had to appeal to the pope for absolution, which the bishop pronounced on condition that he promised to go on crusade when one should be organised (Droxford, p. 65). Simon continued to fight regularly for the king in Wales, Gascony and Scotland and served in Parliament from 1299 as Lord Montagu. Droxford's register records him appointed jointly with the rector of Yarlington as custodian of the nunnery at Whitehall, Ilchester, in 1315, and as taking the rector into his service shortly before his death in 1316 (Droxford, pp. 96, 112). Only in 1313 had he received the king's permission to fortify his house at Yarlington[3], creating the moat that still partly survives.

Simon's son, another William, like his father was employed in Scotland, Wales and abroad from as early as 1301.[4] In Droxford's register he is found choosing rectors for Chedzoy in 1318 and 1319, the last of whom, Walkelin de Ashmorebrook, he took with him to Gascony where he had been appointed Seneschal in the previous year (Droxford, pp. 20, 135, 137–80). William died in Gascony less than a year later[5] and Walkelin, as one of his executors with William's widow and heir, was still involved several years later (Droxford, pp. 143, 147, 194, 241–15). Elizabeth, Lady Montagu, incidentally, appears twice more in

---

[1] G.E.C., *Complete Peerage*, ix, ed. H.A. Doubleday and Lord Howard de Walden (London, 1936), 78.
[2] *Ibid.*
[3] *Ibid.* 79.
[4] *Ibid.* 80–1.
[5] *Ibid.* 82.

the register, as sponsor, and perhaps financier, of two clergymen leaving their parishes to study, one of them the rector of Donyatt where she probably lived in her widowhood (Droxford, pp. 114, 149).

William's namesake and heir, who appears more frequently in Bishop Ralph's register, is recorded in Droxford's time as still under age in 1321 and as patron of Yarlington in 1324 (Droxford, pp. 194, 232). He began his distinguished military and diplomatic career in 1325, was created earl of Salisbury in 1337 and died in 1344.[1] He was said in a papal bull of 1330 copied into Bishop Ralph's register to have been an ambassador to the pope, 1339 as Marshal of England to have been abroad, and in 1343 to be 'in remote parts.' At home he chose rectors for Donyatt in 1334, for Yarlington in 1341 and 1342 and he perhaps rebuilt the private chapel at Donyatt his great-grandfather had built. Bishop Ralph licensed Bishop Grandisson of Exeter, the earl's brother-in-law, to consecrate an altar there in 1339 (Ralph, nos. 216, 733, 1368, 1391, 1572, 1661, 1720, 1744). He is also recorded in the register as founding a priory at his home at Bisham in Berkshire (Ralph, no. 1595). Countess Katherine, Grandisson's youngest sister, took the rector of Exton into her household in 1331 and after her husband's death chose the new rector of Donyatt in 1347 (Ralph, nos. 307, 2006).

William Montague, 2nd earl of Salisbury, is very frequently named in Bishop Ralph's register because the Black Death required new clergy not only in Chedzoy but in the parishes of Montacute, Odcombe, Closworth and Tintinhull that belonged to Montacute priory, whose property was in his hands because of the war with France (Ralph, nos. 2072, 2141, 2222, 2289, 2296, 2371, 2384, 2419, 2483, 2476). Writing from his house at Donyatt, he freed one of his Chedzoy serfs in 1350 and agreed to the union of Curry Rivel and Earnshill parishes in 1353 (Ralph, nos. 2412, 2788). The loss of registers during the rest of the earl's lifetime means his local church activities are for ever unknown.

There were two more Montague earls of Salisbury after Earl William's death in 1397: his nephew John, executed in 1400, and

---

[1] *Ibid*. xi, ed. G.H. White (London, 1949), 385–8.

John's son Thomas, who died of wounds in France in 1428. Earl Thomas could not deal with the vacancy at Chedzoy in 1417 because he was 'in Normandy in the king's service' (Bubwith, no. 723). Before that his great-aunt, Countess Elizabeth, chose the rectors of Goathill in 1406 and of Chedzoy in 1414 (Bowet, no. 240; Bubwith, no. 471). In 1427, when he appointed a rector of Chedzoy again, Thomas was described as earl of Salisbury, count of Perche (created 1419) and lord of Monthermer, a title inherited from his grandmother (Stafford, no. 1333).[1]

On Earl Thomas's death his title and lands passed to his only daughter Alice and to her husband Richard Neville. He, as earl of Salisbury and lord of Monthermer, presented rectors to Goathill, Donyatt and Yarlington at vacancies between 1435 and 1457 (Stafford, nos. 504, 679, 851; Bekynton, nos. 675, 725, 905, 1035, 1085). His death, as one of the leading Yorkists, at or after the battle of Wakefield in 1460 was followed by the loss of the Montague estate, but with the Yorkists in power it was restored to the countess, who presented at the next vacancy at Yarlington in 1462 (Bekynton, no. 1421). The countess died soon afterwards, when the direct Montague line came to an end;[2] she was succeeded by her son Richard Neville, better known as earl of Warwick and better still as Warwick the Kingmaker, who appointed the next rector of Yarlington; the rector of Donyatt appointed by his father, outlived him (Bekynton, nos. 1085, 1552; Stillington & Fox, no. 378). Warwick (died 1471) was succeeded by his daughter Isabel, wife of George, duke of Clarence, and his properties passed to his grandson Edward, earl of Warwick, and in 1499 to the Crown. His granddaughter Margaret, widow of Sir William Pole, regained the family estate in 1513–14 and she, as countess of Salisbury, nominated a rector of Donyatt in 1514 and another in 1523 (King & Hadrian, no, 1046; Wolsey, etc, no. 155). Her execution in 1541 brought a final end to the family. A younger branch of the Montagues, of more modest means and no title had, almost in parallel, presented to the churches of Sutton Montis (or Montagu) and Weston Bampfylde, Sutton from 1342,

---

[1] *Ibid.* 391.
[2] *Ibid.* 398.

Weston from 1310, and continued to do so ending in the death of Robert Montague in 1509 (Droxford, p. 29; Ralph, no. 1694).[1]

An equally modest family was connected with a single church for a similar period. The tiny parish of Seaborough, now in Dorset but part of the minster parish of Crewkerne, was provided with a new rector by John Golde in 1341 (Ralph, no. 1645). A Robert Golde, perhaps three generations later, presented one in 1404 (Bowet, no. 192). A John Golde and his wife were present in what seems to have been a new chapel attached to the parish church in 1415; another Robert appointed a rector in 1436, a Thomas presented in 1465; Thomas, described as esquire, in 1480, and a Thomas in 1523 (Bubwith, no. 563; Stafford, no. 583). The last was the Thomas who died in 1525 and whose son John, lacking male heirs, was murdered in 1555.[2]

8 *Memorial brass to Thomas Golde, esquire, 1525, Crewkerne church: reproduced from A.B. Connor,* Monumental Brasses in Somerset *(Kingsmead Reprints, Bath, 1970), plate lxi*

---

[1] *A History of the County of Somerset (V.C.H.)*, xi, ed. M.C. Siraut (Boydell & Brewer, 2015), 191, 211.

[2] Collinson, *History of the County of Somerset*, ii. 172; *The Particular Description of the County of Somerset*, ed. E.H. Bates (S.R.S. xv, 1900), 134.

CHAPTER III
THE CLERGY AND THEIR PARISHES

The bishop, as 'Father-in-God', was ultimately responsible for the safety of the souls of the people of his diocese, though he obviously depended heavily on the clergy in the parishes. Many entries in the registers involved the legalistic business of the appointment of rectors and vicars, of ensuring that they were adequately qualified, of removing those that were not, and of providing for those who could no longer carry out their duties. The clergy were themselves created by bishops, who first made them tonsurati *(wearers of the distinctive clerical haircut) as promising youths and advanced them through acolyte, sub-deacon, and deacon to ordained priest able to offer the Sacraments of Baptism, Absolution, Matrimony, Eucharist and Extreme Unction. The Sacrament of Confirmation, the remaining Sacrament, could only be administered by a bishop. Walter de Chilterne appeared at Sutton Montis in 1336 to answer the charge of interrupting Bishop Ralph as he anointed some young people (Ralph no 989).*

The making of a clerk (clergyman)
'Good opinion', 'honest conversation', 'good character and legitimate birth', 'knowledge', 'character and birth', 'morals and behaviour' were all phrases used when men wished to become part of what was called the 'clerical army' and presented themselves before a bishop to be ordained – first to be tonsured (given the recognised clerical haircut by the bishop's barber) and then in due course made acolyte, sub-deacon, deacon and priest (Giffard & Bowett no. i; Bekynton nos. 272, 335–6, 681). Character references or recommendations came first; and then the question of birth, whether free (that is, not a serf tied to a manor) and legitimate (born of a married couple). Both those conditions

might be overcome for a suitable candidate but the man born a serf was probably always destined to remain in a modest position. Bishop Droxford freed at least 25 men from serfdom on his estates and tonsured them, usually on condition that they continued to serve him or his successor as bishop. In a single year, 1325, Adam Roules of Wick St Lawrence, 'serf and poor scholar,' was tonsured and had official letters (letters dimissory) to seek further orders from any other bishop, but was obliged to work in his native diocese if he were to be priested. Thomas of Dultecote in the same year had similar letters, but because his father was a burgess of Wells, he was free to find work anywhere; and the rector of Berrow recommended two of his parishioners for tonsuring (Droxford pp. 237–8, 248).

Proof of ordination was obviously of importance when an appointment was to be made. In an extreme case, in 1314 or 1315, Peter de Condray, a priest from Poitou in France, had evidently lost important paper work and had to bring witnesses before Bishop Droxford to prove he had been ordained by Bishop Peter Quinel of Exeter, acting on letters from Bishop Robert Burnell of Bath & Wells (bishop 1275–92). Only then did Droxford give him new proof of his clerical status in writing (Droxford p. 150).

Becoming a rector or vicar
Clerks were appointed to parishes by a standard legal procedure recorded in the registers – presentation (nomination) by a patron, institution (handing over the responsibility for the souls of parishioners) or collation when the patron was a bishop; and institution (giving the clergyman his source of income) by the archdeacon. These were the men, rectors or vicars depending on the status of the appointment they held, whose names may well appear in lists framed and hanging in churches today.

The key to starting the procedure was finding a patron. It is easy to guess how Matthew de Clyvedon came to be made rector of the rich benefice of Aller in 1325, because the patron was his uncle Sir Matthew de Clyvedon; and both his father, Sir John de Clyvedon and his uncle were close associates of Bishop Droxford. It might be reasonable to guess that the prior of Bruton knew Nicholas de Batecomb as a native of the village of Batcombe (and he might even have been taught at the priory school), and saw him as a suitable vicar to serve for them at South Petherton in 1333 (Droxford pp. 211, 293; Ralph no 571). Connections between other candidates and patrons are impossible to fathom, and when they involved people unknown to the bishop called for care. Hence, the bureaucratic rigmarole when in 1323 Richard de Rypon, acolyte, was presented to the tiny parish of St John, Ilchester, by the king. The bishop received the king's letter of presentation, together with a certificate from the archbishop of York's senior official, declaring that the previous rector had died, presumably somewhere in the North, and another certificate from the same official declaring that Richard was free, legitimate, aged 26, able to read, held no other parish, and that there was no legal impediment to his appointment. A further letter, from the dean and chapter of Ripon, attested to Richard's suitable conversation. There was even a covering letter, approving all this correspondence, from the archbishop of York. The chances are that Richard de Rypon never left Yorkshire, but because he now had a Somerset parish, he was in the care of Bishop Droxford, and it was to Droxford that he had to apply for letters dimissory, eventually to be made a priest by any willing bishop (Droxford pp. 218, 221–2). In the 15th century a sure way to promotion was still through birth or education: John Stafford, successively bishop of Bath & Wells and archbishop of Canterbury, was the illegitimate son of a Wiltshire landowner; Thomas Bekynton was said to have been the son of a Beckington weaver, but managed to become a pupil of Winchester College, a student and later fellow of New College, Oxford, a scholar of international fame and a senior civil servant.[1]

The care of the parish

Men duly appointed to parishes had serious obligations. It was their responsibility to offer their parishioners the rites of Baptism, Confession, Eucharist (the Mass), Matrimony and Extreme Unction, or if they were neither deacons nor priests, and were also without sufficient education, to employ other clerks to serve

---

[1] A.F. Judd, *The Life of Thomas Bekynton* (Marc Fitch Fund, 1961).

for them. Such a situation seems to have been quite common, but was rarely mentioned in the registers as the bishop's permission seems not to have been needed unless absence from the parish was involved. Permission to be absent for study or to serve in the household of a patron was commonly given (for a fee), especially in the earlier 14th century.

Leave for study, usually for a year at a time, was granted to as many as 17 men in 1318–19; to many fewer a century later. Roger Pykeslegh, rector of Weston-super-Mare, managed at least seven years away 1311–18, his brother William, of Backwell, at least six, and a third brother Adam, of Hutton, at least five (Droxford pp. 18, 46–7, 54, 78, 82, 163, 305). Walter, rector of Exton, had a single licence for seven years at Oxford 'or elsewhere' from 1315; Henry de Bois, of Timsbury, a year in Paris in 1311 (Droxford pp. 42, 83). Laurence Delabeare, rector of Compton Martin, was more ambitious. He first took leave in 1316, served the papal nuncio in 1317 and was rewarded with a prebend (an income and a place in Quire and Chapter) in Wells cathedral. He took further leave in 1321 for a year, which was extended so he could teach Canon Law at Oxford at least until 1324. He went on to become Droxford's Official (Droxford pp. 11, 169, 275, 306–9). Among the clergy-students a century later, were John Bernard,[1] rector of Claverton, absent 1410–13, later Bishop Stafford's Official and Bishop Bekynton's Vicar-General (his deputy). Stafford[2] himself was licensed in 1413 for one of five years when rector of Farmborough, was Bubwith's successor (Bubwith nos. 62, 270, 337, 429, 432) and later archbishop of Canterbury.

There were, however, conditions attached to licences. Every parish so deprived of its pastor had to be cared for while he was away, and Bekynton spelt out the details to Edmund Warcop, rector of Hutton, in 1443: he might find someone suitable to be tenant of the living:

---

[1] *Ibid.* i. 176–7.
[2] *Ibid.* iii. 1750–2.

provided that divine service and the cure of souls be not neglected, that a suitable proctor (substitute) be left there to answer duly in his behalf to the bishop and his ministers, and that compensation be made for his absence by a distribution of alms among his poor parishioners (Bekynton no. 13).

Walter, rector of Meare in 1331, among others had to return to his parish in Lent, to hear confessions. The rector of North Cadbury in 1332 also had to return for the bishop's visitation. One student cleric, Thomas, rector of Oake in 1341, had to show the bishop his tutors' reports each year (Ralph nos. 343, 422, 1635).

The need for study was clear. In 1316, Droxford admitted a new rector to Holton, but urged him 'to have with him a good chaplain from whom he could learn because he is only poorly educated.' In 1321, as a 'favour,' the bishop gave John Attemede the rectory of Seavington St Michael, and at the same time leave to go to Oxford for 3½ years because he was 'insufficient in learning and for the direction of souls.' The ill-educated new and young rector of Walton in Gordano in 1321 had to study, but also to contribute from his income to towards needy fellow-scholars (Droxford pp. 119, 187, 200). Bishop Bekynton, perhaps the most scholarly bishop of the diocese in the later Middle Ages, seems to have sent far fewer men on study leave than both Droxford and Ralph – only 18 in just over twenty years, several of them already graduates, including John Payne,[1] rector of Walton in Gordano, who ran a student hall of residence in Oxford. And among the others was the new rector of Sutton Bingham, Hugh Wylkyns, not old enough to take Holy Orders but 'on account of his intelligence and his desire to attend the schools' and also because his parish had no inhabitants, was allowed to leave 'so he may make better progress in letters'. As an alternative, Bekynton sometimes intervened earlier in the process, withholding ordination until improvement was demonstrated. Thus, when Thomas Ewley from Worcester diocese came to Wells in March 1463, Bekynton made him a sub-deacon only

---

[1] *Ibid.* iii. 1440–1.

after the rector of Beckington[1] promised to 'render him capable' before being promoted. Perhaps his education took place at the school at Westbury (-on-Trym) college where the rector taught with Bekynton's permission from later the same year (Bekynton nos. 156, 775, 1524, 1778). Among the men most in need of help, but evidently able to afford it, was John Gernesey, the new vicar of Banwell in 1444 who:

> swore on the Gospels that for a whole year he would study every day to understand his divine office and daily service literally and grammatically at least, and during that year maintain in his house at his own expense a young man well-learned in grammar to instruct him (Bekynton no. 73).

He seems already to have been a vicar-choral in the cathedral. Does his name suggest his native language was French?

Bishops also allowed men to be employed far from their parishes by people of influence, though how clerk and patron came to know each other would be a fascinating study. Thomas de Granden, another rector of Seavington St Michael, was required from 1315, probably until her death in 1320, by the dowager countess of Gloucester,[2] the king's niece by marriage; the rector of Charlton Musgrove was called in 1344 'to follow in the service of the king'; and the rector of Chilton Cantelo from 1362 to serve the Prince of Wales (Droxford p. 86; Ralph nos. 1862, *36). The bishops of Salisbury, Worcester and Hereford called for Somerset clergy in Bishop Ralph's time, as did local magnates such as the Courtenays (Ralph nos. 293, 443, 494, 619, 705, 2561, 2783).

There were other, very specific, reasons for absence. William of Bath, rector of Swainswick, was allowed in 1318 to lease his church for two years to a suitable substitute and serve instead as a vicar-choral at Wells 'on account of the ill-will of some of

---

[1] The rector of Beckington was Roger Fabell, rector 1459–73: Emden, *Oxford to 1500*, ii. 663.

[2] Maud de Burgh: G.E.C. *Complete Peerage*, v, ed. V. Gibbs and H.A. Doubleday (London, 1926), 714–15.

his flock'; the rector of Shepton Beauchamp left his parish for two years from 1323 'on account of parochial strife, not caused by him'; and the rectors of Spaxton and Witheridge (in Exeter diocese) found it convenient to exchange parishes in 1362, because the former had fallen out with his near neighbour and patron, and the latter found his job too difficult to do while working for the bishop of Bath & Wells (Droxford pp. 10, 219; Ralph no.*114).

One clerk, clearly with influence and enough money to get himself out of trouble, was the rector of Halse, Stephen atte Putte. Armed with a papal indulgence he was forgiven for acquiring holy orders irregularly, for assaulting a fellow cleric, conducting clandestine marriages and 'other sins' (Droxford p. 118).

The problem of retirement

Once a clerk acquired a rectory or vicarage, he was naturally reluctant to give it up at a time when there was no retirement age and no national pension. The result was often that bishops had to step in when parishioners were obviously suffering the consequences of their priest's incapacity. In Droxford's register six men were described as aged, two aged and ill, two aged and blind, two blind and aged, one blind and disabled, two decrepit, one mad, one out of his mind and one worn out (Droxford pp, 38, 40, 49–50, 92, 102, 107, 111, 114, 123, 127, 129, 166, 177, 207, 209, 233, 255, 259, 262, 275, 278, 282). Coadjutors were often appointed, which left the incumbent at least temporarily in post (e.g. Droxford p. 102; Bekynton nos. 1172, 1299), and pensions and accommodation were arranged. Surely the most deserving of pensioners was Philip Melles,[1] formerly vicar of Wedmore, who was at first in 1446 simply assigned a small house attached to his former home to accommodate himself and his servants, with access to the rest of the building and the garden and the usual sum of 10 marks (£6 13s 4d). But when the new vicar admitted that Philip had paid for his university education,

---

[1] Philip Melles had been vicar of Wedmore since 1418. Four years earlier he seems to have been forced to resign the vicarage of Huish and Langport, when he said he was a priest (Bubwith nos. 508, 767).

the bishop increased the pension to £8. Alternatively, Thomas Drayton, rector of Lydeard St Lawrence, 'on account of his bodily weakness and defective sight', was allowed to let his glebe farm to suitable tenants and put his parishioners in the hands a deputy 'provided in the meantime divine service and the cure of souls be not neglected' (Bekynton nos. 192, 201, 532).

Assistant clergy
Those clergy in possession of parishes, whatever problems of age or physical difficulties, were privileged when compared with a much larger number, who for much of our period are little more than names. They come into their own only from 1450 when they were taxed for the first time. Usually described either as parochial chaplains (in Redcliffe deanery as a parish priest), anniversary chaplains or chaplains of a chantry, the names of 268 men are recorded. It seems likely that the parochial chaplains were in effect the poorly-paid substitutes for absentee rectors and vicars whom influence had brought them a benefice and the chance of a university degree, but who had no interest in becoming a priest or of acting as a permanent pastor of their flock. Their comfortable livings depended on the services of one or more chaplains on whose fell, as one outspoken but distinguished historian declared, 'most of the ill-paid dirty work of the church'.[1]

Such men appear only occasionally in the earlier registers for unusual reasons. In 1317 Richard le Ffrie, described as a priest of Whitelackington (which must mean acting in place of the vicar) found his qualifications questioned. On enquiry, the bishop found that his illegitimacy had been dispensed by papal letters, that his character was approved, that his title, from the parish of Huish Champflower (where he may previously have served) was acceptable, but that he had not sought the bishop's approval before being ordained 'beyond sea'. He was, however, forgiven and was permitted to hold a benefice (Droxford p. 119). No further trace of him is found in the registers of Droxford or Ralph.

---

[1] K.B. McFarlane, *John Wycliffe and the Beginnings of English Nonconformity* (London, 1952), 14.

Three assistant clergy were found at Chedzoy in 1318: an unnamed chaplain, a parish clerk (a holy-water carrier was his official title) called Nicholas Atteslape, who was neither literate nor tonsured, and Nicholas's replacement, known only as Attemore, who was both (Droxford p. 13).

Another, obviously much valued man, was the parish chaplain at Wellington, who received what would now be called a glowing reference from Bishop Ralph in 1333 which was thought so remarkable as to be entered in the register. The bishop declared that Richard Dauid of Buckingham, priest, had served faithfully and worthily in the parish church of Wellington for 24 years and that he was now leaving to return home with hope and good wishes (Ralph no. 608).

More than a century later John Benet was given leave by Bishop Bekynton to take life a little easier: he was eighty and had served 'laudably' in the chantry in Crewkerne and had been choirmaster for over 33 years,[1] but in 1459 realised that daily attendance put a strain on his health (Bekynton no. 1258). Benet, of course, had been one of the four chaplains at Crewkerne who were taxed in 1450. There were in that year three similar chaplains at Wellington, six each at Temple (Bristol), Frome, Yeovil and St Cuthbert's, Wells, nine at Bridgwater, twelve at St Mary's, Taunton (Bekynton, nos. 486–8).

All these and many more chaplains had little hope of further advancement but served their communities almost without record, usually without name. Thus, when in 1343 the parishioners of Chard were allowed to have weekly Mass celebrated in their chapel of Holy Cross in the centre of their developing town, they would have paid a priest to do so (Ralph no. 1779). So would the villagers of Churchill in 1419 after their parish chaplain was permitted to say Mass on a portable altar (Bubwith no. 827). The offerings of the people of Bruton would have supported William Saundford when, with the bishop's permission, he heard the confessions of parishioners during Lent 1403 (Giffard & Bowett

---

[1] He had been at Crewkerne at least since 1422, having been ordained acolyte in 1417, sub-deacon 1419, deacon and priest 1420 (Bubwith, nos. 1098, 1300, 1304–6).

no. 109). The vicars of Kingsbury (Episcopi) after 1447 were expected, as a matter of course, to employ a chaplain and two clerks; and a similar assistant priest must have been left to say Mass at Lydeard St Lawrence in 1450 when the rector was given leave of absence because of ill-health and poor eyesight. Such a man, too, was the parochial chaplain of Uphill, whose rector remembered him in his will in 1457[1] (Bekynton nos. 296, 532, 1053n). The anonymous 'curates' of Winford mentioned in 1499, of Hornblotton in 1505, of Saltford also in 1505 and of Backwell in 1511 were obviously in charge of those parishes when their rectors were absent. Equally anonymous curates of Publow and St Cuthbert's, Wells, were addressed in 1499 and 1502 about weddings in their churches (King & Hadrian nos. 161, 254, 427, 649, 658, 922).

---

[1] Emden, *Oxford to 1500*, i. 235.

CHAPTER IV
MONASTERIES AND NUNNERIES

Monasteries, some of them founded in Saxon times, were important in Somerset's history in many ways: places of prayer and spiritual power, centres of learning, owners and developers of huge parts of the landscape, sources of place-names like Hinton Charterhouse, Witham Friary, Minchin Buckland or Buckland Sororum. They were also usually small, enclosed communities of human beings where relationships could become strained and where the original hopes of founders could be difficult to achieve. Bishops, hearing the criticisms of neighbours and asking awkward questions, probably discovered and recorded the worst.

Bishops were responsible in a general way for the monasteries in their dioceses, though they were excluded from formally visiting those of the Cluniac, Cistercian and Carthusian Orders (in Bath & Wells, Montacute; Cleeve; Hinton and Witham) and were usually not very welcomed by the enormously rich and powerful Glastonbury. But bishops were involved in elections of heads of houses and were essential in the ordination of monks and canons. Visitations involved the bishop or his deputies asking each member of a community in turn and probably in private, to declare anything they had to complain about, a process that often gave rise to negative responses, and occasionally raised the possibility that oaths of secrecy had been taken in advance to cover up any problems.[1] Most registers include what were originally separate records of elections, which include the names of monks, canons

---

[1] The inference drawn in Droxford, p. 153 that such an oath had been taken at Bath and Glastonbury is based on a misreading of the marginal entry, which describes an oath to tell the truth before the visitation.

or nuns present on each occasion. Bishops often recorded their recommendations for improvement after visitation, giving interesting clues as to what they found to be wrong.

No such records of problems survive from Droxford's time, but he obviously visited (enquired into) Bath, Glastonbury, Muchelney, Stoke (sub Hamdon) college, Cannington and Barrow (Droxford pp. 93, 153, 159, 185, 217, 238, 245, 289). There are references to elections, for instance at Barlinch, Barrow and Stogursey; to the ordination of men from, for example, Hinton and Keynsham; and many more to poverty or poor administration (Keynsham from damage to estates in Wales and Ireland, Muchelney because of flooding, Barrow and Whitehall in Ilchester due to incompetence (Droxford pp. 8, 32, 45, 93, 96, 115, 168, 177–8, 228, 240, 294). 'Illicit wandering' of nuns from Cannington and the transfer of a canon from Taunton to Keynsham and perhaps two from Woodspring to Bruton for proper penance for misbehaviour (Droxford pp. 90, 103, 172–3, 289) shows that all was not well everywhere; but Muchelney was considered by the bishop of Lincoln a suitable place for punishment for a Peterborough monk sentenced to solitary in fetters in 1314. He was returned in 1319, having escaped twice (Droxford p. 8). Practical consequences of poverty were that Athelney abbey's church was so ruinous the monks had to resort to public collections; and Woodspring was thought to avoid fees by not asking the bishop to consecrate their new church (Droxford pp. 171, 189).

Bishop Ralph left detailed criticism of life at Muchelney in 1335, at Glastonbury in 1350 and at Cannington in 1351. Life at Muchelney, he thought, was luxurious and privileged, although the abbey church was in great need of repair. The liturgy at Glastonbury he found to be rather lax, the food not good and the abbot distant from his monks. At Cannington, one nun was discovered pregnant, two more (one who had been recommended by the bishop himself) had behaved in unseemly fashion with two chaplains, the prioress had admitted four sisters in return for money and the sub-prioress had missed church services and failed in her duties. All were duly punished (Ralph nos. 101, 570, 788, 2328, 2607, 2629). The election of a new prioress in 1336 was recorded in full, including the way each member of the 14-strong community voted, all expressed in correct and lengthy legal form. An election at Taunton in 1339 was similarly recorded in detail (Ralph nos. 1071, 1332).

Bishop Bubwith or his registrar thought the sentence against the unsatisfactory Prior Shoyll of Bruton should be entered in the register in 1423, and the shortcomings of the priory were exposed in Bishop Stafford's injunctions in 1425 (Bubwith no. 1191; Stafford no. 264). Bekynton, keener than most of his fellows to improve monastic standards, recorded his directions for improvement for Taunton, Muchelney and Keynsham after visitations in 1451, for Muchelney, Athelney and Keynsham in 1455, and for St John's hospital, Bridgwater, in 1463. Deputies were sent to Taunton, Muchelney, Athelney and Keynsham in 1458 because the bishop had heard that his earlier instructions had been ignored (Bekynton nos. 578, 582, 586, 654, 707, 936–7, 957, 1159, 1514). Bekynton also recorded monastic elections with great care (Bekynton nos. 1636–51) and so did his successors with the exception of Wolsey, until 1525 (Stillington & Fox nos. 996–9, 1168–77; King & Hadrian nos. 515–22, 1171–8; Wolsey, etc. nos. 473–79).

Stillington, hearing a 'common report' that the abbot of Glastonbury had been 'careless and negligent in matters both spiritual and temporal', went so far as to appoint a fellow bishop, and two archdeacons and a canon from other dioceses, to visit the abbey in 1472. He abandoned a general personal visitation of his diocese in 1477 because of his government duties and appointed officers to take his place in April 1477 (Stillington & Fox nos. 393, 547, 634–6, 647). No other record of monastic visitation is to be found in the registers, but a record of visitations by Bishop Clerke's vicar-general of St John's hospital, Wells, Glastonbury, Barrow, St John's hospital, Bristol, Keynsham, Bruton, Muchelney, Athelney, Taunton, Barlinch, Cannington, St John's hospital, Bridgwater, and Woodspring in 1526, and another of Glastonbury and Athelney in 1538 have survived, not entered in the general register as they would have been earlier, but still fortunately kept safely among the bishops' records.[1]

---

[1] '*Visitation of Religious Houses and Hospitals, 1526*', ed. H. Maxwell Lyte, In *Collectanea I*, ed. T.F. Palmer (S.R.S. xxxix, 1924), 207–25; *Dean*

Individual members of religious houses were recorded as each bishop considered necessary. William de Warwyc, William de Grandcombe or Crowcombe, Richard Engayne and Richard de Colingham, formerly Templars turned out of their home at Templecombe in 1309 and treated as prisoners for offences they and their Order were accused of by the king, were later lodged respectively in Glastonbury, Muchelney, Taunton and Montacute at the Crown's expense. William of Crowcombe became a Benedictine monk in 1319 (Droxford pp. 98, 137). Prior John Iford of Bath had an affair with a woman from Gloucestershire in 1346 and Henry Brikebet joined the community of Glastonbury in 1361 probably to avoid marriage (see Chapter VI) (Ralph nos. 1962, 14*). Prior John Shoyll of Bruton was evidently induced to resign by Bishop Stafford in 1430, but he was a disruptive influence in his retirement, and after a year was sent to a tiny priory in the Berkshire Downs (Stafford nos. 289, 307, 933). Bishop Bekynton fell out seriously with Abbot Nicholas Frome of Glastonbury after finding problems at his first visitation (Bekynton nos. 120, 133). The correspondence between the two was kept private[1] and was never entered into the register.

The appointment of Richard Beere as abbot of Glastonbury in 1494 did not involve the usual grand and formal ceremony. The election of Thomas Wasyn (perhaps because the bishop's permission to elect had not been sought) was annulled and Beere was appointed by Bishop Fox alone, and in a much simpler ceremony in Doulting church he made his oath of obedience to the bishop (Stillington & Fox nos. 1175–7).

There are no entries about monks or monasteries in Bishop Clerk's register after June 1534, and by the beginning of Bishop Knyght's rule in May 1541 the monasteries had been dissolved. Only echoes survive, such as the presentation of a new vicar of Englishcombe in the following June by a group of men to whom, while he still had power, William Byrde, prior of Bath, had

---

Cosyn and Wells Cathedral Miscellanea, ed. A. Watkin (S.R.S. lvi, 1941), 159–65.

[1] *Official Correspondence of Thomas Bekynton*, ed. G. Williams (Rolls Series, 1872), i. pp. 258–9; ii. pp. 338–9.

conveyed the right of appointment. A similar one was made at Pitminster by a group authorised by the prior of Taunton 'lately dissolved' (Wolsey, etc. nos. 468–9, 481, 485, 491).

CHAPTER V
THE ORDINARY, THE DEVOUT AND THE QUESTIONING

There were, in every age, men and women with varying religious awareness. Most were ordinary folk with a simple faith, whose prayers were valued and whose offerings and practical assistance were essential to every clergyman serving in a parish and to the fabric of every church. Some few, experiencing their faith more deeply, looked to get way from the world alone, rather than in a religious community; a few more went on pilgrimage. Hermits and pilgrims needed the formal support of their bishop. And, of course, there were those who had doubts and were bold enough to give voice to them.

People of Faith

The registers are not concerned with how the clergy actually taught their people, though Bishop Stafford supported the king's wish that they should rehearse 'openly in English to the people without curious subtiltee' the Creed, the Ten Commandments, the Seven Works of Mercy, the Seven Deadly Sins, the Seven Principal Virtues and the Seven Sacraments (Stafford, no. 511). Clergy unable to teach for lack of education themselves had to find someone who could (see Chapter III). Sunday mass 'when the number of people present is largest' (Stafford no. 509) was the principal service of the week, and among the feasts of the Church, Christmas, Easter and those of the patron and of the building's consecration were most popular. In the 15th century, sometimes perhaps owing to pressure on harvest labour, dedication days were changed to dates when the number of participants (and therefore of gifts) might be maximised (see Chapter VIII). Changes elsewhere are more difficult to understand. At Croscombe the change in 1422 was from 11 to 19 October, at Kingstone in 1450 from 1 February to the first Sunday in October, and at West Cranmore in 1525 the date, almost at the last moment, was altered from Friday January 13 to the octave of the Epiphany (eighth day after January 6), that is by a day! (Bubwith no. 1127; Bekynton no. 528; Wolsey, etc. no. 214).

Medieval religion is seen in the registers as both passive and active: simple presence at mass in church but regular attendance at processions outside. By an 'ancient tradition' the rector of North Cadbury processed around a detached part of Blackford within his parish long before the Black Death (Bubwith no. 543), and in 1336 a new vicarage house was built at Bathampton at the eastern side of the churchyard 'by the processional way' (Ralph no. 1084). Regular processions were still assumed to be taking place in the 15th century across the country, though the response to a national request for prayers at the same time in 1416 was 'lukewarm' and the request was repeated 'to incite the faithful to pray more devoutly' (Bubwith no. 645). In November 1462 Bekynton requested litanies (chanted prayers) 'during the coming weeks' around churches (inside or outside is not clear) on Wednesdays and Fridays (Bekynton no. 1464). Seventy years later, when the need for them had apparently grown, clergy were expected to recite public prayers daily in all churches, and lay people had to join them on Mondays, Wednesdays and Fridays in cities, boroughs and 'important places.' Responses were evidently not good: the king heard that processions were attended 'verie slacklie' (Wolsey, etc. nos. 417, 583).

Private prayers combined with pilgrimage were encouraged. In 1464 contrite and confessed people were offered indulgences to visit the tomb of the Carents at Henstridge and there say *Pater Noster* (Lord's Prayer) and *Ave Maria* (Hail Mary) for the family. A similar offer, from Archbishop Stafford and nine bishops including Bekynton in 1452 for gifts for the relocation of the miracle-working image and altar at Old Cleeve (Bekynton nos. 648, 934, 1568) was just one of 45 for what would now be called crowd-funding that are to be frequently found in the registers for causes across the country and beyond (see Appendix II).

And was it simple devotion or superstition that caused the sudden popularity of St John's spring at Wembdon church in 1464; or the vision of blood coming from a loaf of bread as John Strange of Porlock paused while cutting a tree in a wood in 1499 (Bekynton no. 1582; King & Hadrian no. 251)?

The Devout
Some people seem to have created what were called oratories or chapels in their own houses where family or private prayers might be said (see Appendix III). It might have been in a room specially set aside, perhaps in a recess or a window embrasure; anywhere, as some licences declared, 'suitable'. In such spaces, sometimes for understandable reasons of age or illness, sometimes, perhaps, for convenience, sometimes even for a wish to distance themselves from others for social reasons, both men and women applied to the bishop for leave to have mass said privately. Bishops usually put a limit on such permission and were concerned that the parish churches should not suffer from the absence of such substantiaal folk. The licences sometimes specified, when mass was to be said, that the correct liturgical furniture be provided and that the mass be said and not sung.

The licence issued by Bishop Droxford in 1314 to Alice de Horsted at Milborne Wick in the parish of Milborne Port provided for a portable altar, a small, consecrated slab of stone, set up on a wooden table. Bishop Bekynton's new oratory, for which, of course, he needed no formal permission, was recorded by chance as the venue of the ordination of a canon of Taunton in 1456 (Bekynton no. 1732). Part of the decoration of one of its walls is to be found under the floor of one of the Palace bedrooms. The list of places in Appendix III is obviously incomplete: chapels are to be found, for example, in or as part of three houses within a few miles of each other in West Somerset – Gothelney Hall in Charlinch and Blackmoor Farm and Gurney Street, both in Cannington – all of which date to the later years of the 15th century but for which no licence has been found. There are also traces of an oratory at West Bower, a distant part of Bridgwater parish. There William Coker had licence in 1334 to have an oratory because of illness, and his son Richard

9 The chapel in the right wing of Blackmoor Farm, Cannington: engraving, 1859, by A.A. Clarke

another in 1339 (Ralph nos. 729, 1363). More than a century later Bishop Bekynton gave permission for the 'chapel or oratory' there, dedicated to St John the Baptist, to be the place Margaret Hody, nee Coker, married Sir Reynold Stourton early in 1462 (Bekynton no. 1412). One of the turret windows (bearing the initials A and M)[1] might mark the position of that chapel. Margaret's prayer book still survives in a private collection in the United States.

Hermits
Only one Somerset hermit, walled up for twenty-nine years in a cell attached to the little church of Haselbury Plucknett, has any claim to sainthood – St Wulfric of Haselbury – but he

---

[1] The initials of Margaret and of her first husband, Alexander Hody: *Somerset and Dorset Notes and Queries*, xxvii. 55–6.

lived many years before the first surviving register.[1] At least nine hermits are recorded having themselves similarly shut away with their bishops' support and approval. The first was brother Thomas, strictly speaking not a hermit as he lived in a cell with an unnamed companion at Oath in Aller parish from 1328. Bishop Droxford was involved because Thomas wanted his confessor, the vicar of Muchelney, to make a door in his cell and to keep the key to it, presumably an alteration to the original arrangement by Droxford or one of his predecessors (Droxford p. 284). Bishop Ralph approved three hermits: Philip Schipham of Winscombe in 1331, John Worm of Glastonbury in 1335, and the only female in the diocese, Margaret Meifolyne, described as 'old and barren', who was prepared to renounce her marriage to Andrew of Taunton in 1349 (Ralph nos. 279, 934, 2372). Robert Cherde, a monk of Forde, preferred an even more solitary life in 1402 and asked to live in a house at the west end of Crewkerne church (Giffard & Bowett no. 101).[2] After them came Thomas Bourne of Congresbury, who died in or before 1414; Stephen Coye, whose purpose was to collect money for the road from Bristol to Dundry from 1445; and John Crede who, having contracted leprosy, or some other skin complaint, wanted to live in a hermitage at Langley in Selwood Forest from 1448 (Bubwith no. 473, Bekynton nos. 132, 362). Chapels called hermitages were mentioned in Neroche Forest in 1317, at South Cadbury in 1411,[3] and in Crewkerne (dedicated to St Edmund) in 1444 (Droxford p. 167; Bubwith no. 291; Bekynton no. 60). In addition, six people, called neither anchorites nor hermits, made formal vows of chastity: Andrew of Taunton in 1349, John Champflower of Wyke Champflower in 1351, Lady Margaret,

---

[1] *Wulfric of Haselbury, by John, abbot of Ford*, ed. M. Bell (S.R.S. xlvii, 1932).

[2] John Knyght was an anchorite at Crewkerne in 1439: *Supplications from England and Wales in the Registers of the Apostolic Penitentiary, 1410–1503*, ed. Peter D Clarke and Patrick N R Zutshi (Canterbury and York Society 103–5, 2012–15), i, no. 441.

[3] It was occupied by an unnamed hermit in the 1440s: *History of Somerset*, ed. Siraut, xi. 107.

widow of Sir Leonard Hakeluyt in 1413, Eleanor, widow of Thomas Ide of Bruton in 1464 and another widow, Tamsyn Dawbeney in 1506 (Ralph nos. 2372, 2616; Bubwith no. 440; Bekynton no. 1555; King & Hadrian no. 692). Lady Hakeluyt's vow was in the genteel French to which she was probably accustomed; Eleanor Ide could not write, but signed her English vow with a cross and was clothed 'with a widow's habit and the other marks of a widow under vow'; Tamsyn Dawbeney's vow was according to the Rule of St Paul, that is St Paul the Hermit. In addition, Edith, John Champflower's wife, also in 1351 swore a vow of chastity, and promised as soon as possible to become a nun.

Pilgrims
Seven parish clergy received Bishop Droxford's permission to go on pilgrimages. In 1316 the rector of Mells asked leave to go to the shrine of St James at Compostella in company with his patron Lord Monthermer. The rector of Oare and the vicar of Bridgwater went in 1318, the first to Avignon (where he combined pilgrimage with business in the papal court), the other to the shrine of St Thomas at Canterbury. The rector of Bleadon went to Canterbury in the following year and the rector of Bagborough to Compostella. The vicar of St Mary's, Taunton, planned to visit Avignon and unspecified 'foreign shrines.' One layman also asked for the bishop's support. Simon de Montague had already taken an oath to go to the Holy Land, but in 1311 needed the bishop's approval to break his vow because he was in gaol (Droxford pp. 14, 17, 65, 105, 133, 144, 146, 219).

Bishop Ralph gave the rector of Combe Hay leave of absence between January and mid-June 1334 to go on pilgrimage 'beyond seas', and John Champflower of Wyke went to the Holy Land after taking his oath of chastity. Thomas Prowse, prior of Taunton, went to Rome in 1499 'for the benefit of his soul.' Any of those pilgrimages might not have been entirely voluntary. That of Walter, son of Thomas de Spekyngton to 'Compostella and other places' over three years from 1339 was part of his penance for stealing corn from the rector of Yeovilton (Ralph nos. 631, 1378, 2616; King & Hadrian no. 723).

The Questioning

There was another sort of piety. The loss of the registers of bishops Harewell (1369–86), Skirlaw (1386–8) and Erghum (1388–1400) means that the early history of Lollards – the popular name for the followers of John Wycliffe – and of others at the same time who questioned traditional teachings of the Church cannot be told from the beginning in the diocese, though it is certain that Archbishop Courtenay of Canterbury found activists when he came to investigate the dioceses of Worcester and Bath & Wells in 1384, probably all of them in Bristol.[1] Bishop Bubwith found some erroneous preaching there in 1408, and yet more, by a named preacher, John Bacon, formerly a chaplain at Stoke sub Hamdon, in 1412. Bubwith was initially so alarmed that he temporarily placed nine parishes including Crewkerne, Ilminster and Langport under interdict, thus suspending all Church activity including burials (Giffard & Bowett no. 337; Bubwith nos. 94, 338). Bishop Stafford found someone known only as 'Brother William' 'vehemently suspected' of heresy in 1426, but three years later William Emayn, then living in Bristol, caused him more concern and his detailed examination spreads across four pages in his register (Stafford nos. 83, 263).

Emayn had already been examined four times by Philip Repingdon, bishop of Lincoln 1405–19 (and himself a former follower of Wycliffe) in whose diocese he had been born and brought up. Now, under sentence of excommunication and in law liable to execution by burning, he appeared in the Chapter House at Wells on 10 March 1429 before a large audience including Bishop Stafford, the abbot of Glastonbury, the dean of Wells and several canons, two theologians and three lawyers, and made a series of statements of his views in Latin. Four days later he spoke again with the bishop, and his beliefs were then summarised in English: he thought that prayer should be made directly to God and not through saints; that images or pilgrimages or confession or a sinful pope had no value; that Wycliffe and named (and executed) disciples were holy martyrs,

---

[1] *Register of Henry Wakefield, Bishop of Worcester 1375–95*, ed. Marett, xx, no. 775.

Wycliffe himself holier than St Thomas of Canterbury. Ten days later Emayn took it all back, again before a large audience, declaring in English that he had been wrong. He was duly absolved, and nothing further is heard of him. At a similar gathering in 1441 John Jurdayn, also of Bristol, confessed he had been wrong in preaching and teaching against the sacraments of the Church, and in particular that the bread, after consecration, remained bread; a view that came to be at the heart of the Reformation. He, too, retracted all his views and was probably forgiven. Apparently at the same time Thomas Oke, a Taunton brewer, was found in possession of books in English, assumed to have been heretical. Such possession was widely and publicly denounced (Stafford nos. 833–4).

Bishop Bekynton in 1449 heard that 'some' men and women in Bristol and other places in the diocese had been both suspected and accused of heresy, and the appointment of two of his staff as 'inquisitors' was duly registered. One of those suspects was Thomas Yonge, formerly a chaplain of Temple parish, who had been arrested about a year earlier and placed in the keeping of the abbot and prior of Muchelney. He was now old, ill and probably blind but a long-time Lollard and admitted he had caused many people in Bristol to think wrongly. He underwent a very detailed examination on 42 specific points, revealing that he thought the communion service was simply a commemoration, that any man (but not women) might preach, that Rome had no authority, that images should not be venerated, that pilgrimages were not necessary, that tithes should be paid to the poor, that religious orders were of the Devil. Under excommunication, Yonge admitted his errors in detail, confessing that he had possessed and copied from books in English, and finally making the sign of the Cross on his formal abjuration with his thumb and kissing it. That seems to have been the end of the matter (Bekynton nos. 455, 458).

In 1457 Walter Comber, who had lived in St Katherine's hospital in Temple parish, Bristol, was arrested in Portishead. At Banwell he was questioned closely by the bishop who, after hearing his views and the evidence of witnesses, committed him to his prison. Comber had considered William Smyth,[1] burnt some time earlier outside Bristol, a martyr, had declared a priest in sin could not consecrate bread at Mass and that every layman could do so. He then appeared before the bishop's two senior officers and others and retracted his views, realising that he himself was 'in dome (doom) and jugement'. He promised never to hold such opinions again nor consort with anyone who did, and to report such people; and at the foot of his written undertaking, before distinguished witnesses, he made the sign of a cross. He was, presumably, forgiven and allowed to go free (Bekynton no. 1044).

Smyth had been reported by a Gloucester Lollard as the source of a banned book in English.[2] In 1458 Bekynton received from the archbishop of Canterbury, and passed on to his archdeacons, an order to search for people who had either books by Bishop Reginald Pecock (who had been condemned for supporting some Lollard views) or translations of the Bible into English by him or others, such translations seen by the Church authorities as highly dangerous and by Lollards as essential to the understanding of the Faith (Bekynton nos. 1134–5).

Bekynton's last recorded Lollard case was against Thomas Cole or Baker and his wife Agnes, of Norton St Philip. Thomas admitted to saying, among other things, that a man 'in dedly synne' should not say the Lord's Prayer and that praying in the fields was better than in church with an angry neighbour. Agnes thought it was better not to say the Lord's Prayer in anger and spoke against pilgrimages including the Trinity of Bath and St Osmund at Salisbury. Both, having subscribed to their individual abjurations, were to take part as penitents in the procession from the cathedral around the market place and High Street in Wells, and on the following Sunday around the churchyard at Norton St Philip (Bekynton no. 1276).

There followed silence on these matters until January 1476 when two Carthusian monks and six Bath & Wells laymen,

---

[1] A smith of Lawford's Gate, Bristol, 'one of the most active Lollards of his day': J.A.F. Thomson, *The Later Lollards, 1414–1520* (Oxford, 1965), 34.
[2] *Ibid*.

'suspect of heresy and heretical pravity,' were found to have been operating at home, in London and in other southern dioceses. Before witnesses in the house of the dean of St Paul's, a tribunal that included the keeper of the king's Privy Seal and the Clerk of the Rolls, Bishop Stillington handed them over to the archbishop of Canterbury. Less than a month later the bishop appointed three canons of Wells 'to make enquiry with regard to all persons ... who are charged with heretical pravity'. The next day Richard Gryg, a Wrington weaver, formerly thinking along the lines of Thomas Yonge, acknowledged his errors. Later in the year Stephen Freene, John Foregge and John Preste, evidently of Bristol, John Burges of Beckington and Agnes Abraham of Leigh on Mendip (a Roger Habraham was one of the London six) protested their innocence when charged with heresy, so the clergy of Redcliffe, Beckington and Leigh were ordered to call for witnesses (Stillington & Fox nos. 342, 623, 625, 637–8).

Bishop King's visitation (parochial enquiry) in the summer of 1499 produced eleven people, nine (perhaps ten) from Bristol, one from Wells. Two, Nicholas White and Robert Hoton alias Pynner, both of Bristol, proved their innocence, John Shipman, also of Bristol, was absolved. John Walssh of Bristol confessed to believing in three Gods and to have consorted with heretics; Katherine Love of Wells had practised minor sorcery; William Lewys denied that consecrated bread changed to Christ's body; and William Hall of Bristol, examined in the bishop's chapel in the Palace at Wells, denied he taught and preached against pilgrimages and the veneration of saints. John Bouwney the elder, of Redcliffe, abjured, was ordered to do public penance in Wells and Redcliffe, and not to leave the parishes of Temple and Redcliffe without the bishop's permission. William Lewys, after penance, was similarly confined to southern Bristol (King & Hadrian nos. 210, 229, 236–9, 242–3, 289, 298, 334).

The last case of heresy, in the way understood for the previous century and more, and entered in a bishop's register,[1] was that

---

[1] People from Redcliffe and Temple parishes and also from Buckland Dinham, Batcombe and South Cadbury were in trouble, for instance, at a visitation conducted for the king in 1537, one of the Batcombe offenders

of Richard Wytcombe of Holcombe, who confessed that he had made fun of the bread and the chalice at the Mass and was condemned to do public penance in Wells. But silence thereafter does not mean there were no more critics of the Church, and the return of Catholic rule during Queen Mary's reign produced an entry in Bourne's register recording the dismissal of John Taylor alias Cardmaker from the office of chancellor in Wells cathedral. Taylor, a married priest and also vicar of Wellington, was burnt as a heretic in London in 1555 (Wolsey, etc. no. 669 and note).

---

having read from an English New Testament with his neighbours: S.H.C. D/D/Ca 10.

CHAPTER VI
MARRIAGE, DIVORCE AND FAMILY PROBLEMS

The Church was prepared to defend the sacrament of marriage with regulations which were designed to ensure social stability in communities that were often very small and with limited gene pools. Necessary rules confused many people, notably those who were ignorant of what was meant by consanguinity – what relationship between two people would prevent them from marrying each other. Marriages which involved property rather than affection were often doomed to failure, and simple promises were found by some to be inconvenient. Recourse to the church courts was therefore common; those cases that came to the bishop could evidently not be settled there. Only the bishop could declare a marriage null and void, and only a bishop could permit a marriage to be celebrated other than in a parish church.

The cases brought to the attention of the bishops and recorded in their registers vary from the issue of special licences for ceremonies between people of well-known families in their private chapels to breaches of promise which included the misfortune of an abandoned clerical mistress with children. The names Coker, Gorges, Luttrell, Perceval, Seymour, Stawell, St Loe, Stourton and Wadham among the cases below show the social significance of marriage, and those references are contributions to the early genealogies of those families. The importance attached to the public performance of marriages is shown by the number of clandestine ones discovered and corrected.

Marriage, Divorce and Family Problems

The case of the clandestine marriage of Dame Margaret Luttrell, widow of Sir John Luttrell, had wider implications. She was the widow of a tenant-in-chief of the Crown, and her second marriage should have had royal approval. The whole affair, it is clear, was managed by the extravagant lady (her father was Lord Audley of Nether Stowey castle), though evidently not in consultation with Stafford one of the trustees of the family estates. The marriage was entirely valid and only the vicar was in trouble for breaking the rules. Failing to get royal licence cost the bride the huge sum of £40. The marriage itself was not recorded among the family archives.[1]

John Mone in 1511, far from acting secretly, openly boasted: 'I will kepe Johan Brownyng as my wife, my sayd wife being alive, in despite of the churche'. He was arrested, imprisoned and examined by learned clergy and lawyers, and eventually confessed. He was told to avoid the company of Joan Browning and to perform public penance in Wells, Glastonbury, Bridgwater, Ditcheat, Bath and St Mary Redcliffe, carrying a bundle of faggots on his shoulders displaying a clearly legible declaration on paper: 'I have deluded the holy sacrament of matrymony' (Wolsey, etc. no. 20).

The cases below indicate that canon law affected landowners and parkers alike.

Marriage Cases in the Registers:

Hugh or **Henry de Lamplo/Langplo** to divorce **Joan, daughter of Beatrice de Bruys/la Brus**, 1316 (Droxford pp. 100, 113).
Droxford acted as judge for the pope in a suit **Margaret Goatacre** brought against **Robert Selyman** of *Goatacre* (Wilts) for 'want of conjugal affection' 1318 (Droxford p. 12).
The vicar of *Westbury* was punished in 1321 for failing to find a husband for the daughter of the bishop's parker there, by whom he had two children (Droxford p. 166).
John le Perceval married **Millicent Seymour**, but **John Talbot** 'withholds' her, claiming her as his wife, 1329 (Ralph no. 107).

---

[1] H.C. Maxwell Lyte, *A History of Dunster* (London, 1909), i. 114–18.

The vicar of *Winscombe* absolved for celebrating a marriage in a chapel outside the parish church without banns, 1333 (Ralph no. 575).

Licence for **Richard de Stapleton** and **Eleanor de Stawel**, to marry at *Cothelstone* with banns, 1333 (Ralph no. 614).

Maud de Kymyngton was declared to be married to **Thomas de Acton** in a lawsuit she brought against him, 1336 (Ralph no. 981).

The marriage between **Gilbert Ammercy** and **Christiana Underhulle** in *Keynsham* parish church was clandestine, 1337 (Ralph no. 1140).

Licence for **Roger Turtle**, citizen of *Bristol*, and **Juliana, daughter of Margery la Irisch**, to marry in *Badgworth* chapel in *Weare* parish, with banns, 1339 (Ralph no. 1381).

William Peytevyn of *Mells* agrees under bond to permit his wife **Ellen** to live in his house 'honestly and peaceably' and be maintained by him; he will not torment nor chastise her, but she must not commit adultery nor spend their money in luxury, 1342 (Ralph no. 1677).

Licence for **Theobald Gorges** and **Agnes, daughter of John de Wyke**, to marry in the chapel of John de Wyke's house in *Yatton* parish after banns, 1343 (Ralph no. 1751).

John atte Pole called Le Smyth, priest, in ignorance, married **John de Whityngton** and **Joan Lydeneye** by banns called three times within two days. The priest is forgiven 1347 (Ralph no, 2004).

Thomas de Schyrygge and **Eleanor** --- were married in *Nynehead* church on 2 February by Richard Boggere, chaplain, 1349 (Ralph no. 2600).

Licence for **William Teutebury** and **Maud Martel** to be married by Thomas Hulle, chaplain, in the chapel of the house formerly of Canon Richard de Sudbury in *Wells*, 1349 (Ralph no. 2356).

Christian Courtenay brought a matrimonial suit against **Henry Brikebet**, monk of *Glastonbury*, 1361 (Ralph no. *14).

Licence for **William Coker** to marry **Joan, widow of Sir Walter le Irisch** in the chapel of *Milton* in the parish of *Kewstoke*, 1362 (Ralph no. *38).

Robert Nywelond married **Alice** in the chapel of St John Evangelist annexed to parish church of *Curry Mallet* on St Barnabas day 11 June 1403 (Giffard & Bowett 378).

Papal indulgence for **Thomas Poteray** of *Kingston Seymour* and **Alice Hendy** of the same to remain married although they were related in the third or fourth degrees of consanguinity, 1418 (Bubwith no. 804).

William Hunte of *Weryngton* and **Isabel Wille** were given leave to remain married (and their children made legitimate) although Isabel was godchild to Margaret, William's first wife, 1424 (Bubwith no. 1260).

William Estimer alias **Bonde** and **Agnes, widow of William Yonge**, are permitted to remain married (and with legitimate children) as they were not known to be related. Witnesses: Thomas Estimere and Edmund Sordyche), 1430 (Stafford no. 276).

Order to absolve **Robert Coker**, esquire, and **Lady Margaret Luttrell** for their clandestine wedding by the vicar of *Carhampton*, who acted in good faith, 1432 (Stafford no. 355).

John Assh of *Taunton* opposed the claim by **John Bisshop** of *Thorncombe* that he had married **Alice, widow of John Bothe** of *Taunton*, 1434 (Stafford no. 481).

Order for divorce to be decreed between **William Braye** and **Alice Sydenham** of *Milverton*, who had married in Wales, knowing that Alice was godmother to William's illegitimate son **Robert**, 1448 (Bekynton no. 373).

The matrimonial cause brought by **John Gore** the elder of *Kingston* (?St Mary) against **Christine Decon**, daughter of Thomas Decon of the same, to be dealt with quietly, 1453 (Bekynton no 806).

Declaration that **Nicholas Clerk** and **Joan Fitz alias Figis** may remain married although the are related in the fourth degree, 1455 (Bekynton no. 946).

Thomas Combe alias Smyth of *Wells*, a married man, and **Agnes Cole**, also of *Wells*, were excommunicated for adultery and fled to *Exeter*; to be excommunicated there, 1457 (Bekynton no. 1051).

Licence for **Sir Reginald Stourton**, of Salisbury diocese, and **Dame Margaret**, widow of **Sir Alexander Hody**, to be married at the oratory of St John the Baptist at *West Bower*, home of Margaret, by any suitable chaplain; the vicar of *Bridgwater* must approve and call banns, 1462 (Bekynton no. 1412).

Order from the bishop's court, unspecified, to the curate of *Publow*, concerning a marriage between **Henry Gibbys** of *Bath* and **Aline Somerset** of *Publow*, 1499 (King & Hadrian no. 254).

Licence for **Edward Wadham** and **Isabel Seyntlowe**, widow of **Sir John Seyntlowe**, to be married in their oratory at *Bishop's Sutton* in the parish of *Chew Magna* by any secular chaplain, 1500 (King & Hadrian no. 252).

Licence for the curate of St Cuthbert's, *Wells*, to celebrate the marriage of **John Devynshyre** and **Rose Coke**, both of St Cuthbert's, *Wells*, with banns called only twice, 1502 (King & Hadrian no. 427).

Thomas Smyth of *Countisbury* (Devon) and **Joan Buteler** of *Porlock* to be divorced, 1502 (King & Hadrian no. 468).

Isabel Bawdewyn of *East Brent* and **John Grist** of the same to be divorced, 1502 (King & Hadrian no. 468).

Thomas Colyer and **Clemence Arnall**, are permitted by papal authority to marry although his mother was her godmother, 1510 (King & Hadrian no. 907).

In a matrimonial suit between **Joan Holberne** of *Corston* and **John Rede** of *Burnett*, Joan and her father were ordered not to trouble John Rede further, 1511 (King & Hadrian no. 927).

John Mone of *Ditcheat*, who married **Alys Servyngton** and then, bigamously, **Joan Brownyng**, was imprisoned and later sentenced to punishment 1519 (Wolsey, etc. no. 20).

CHAPTER VII
WILLS: THE CHURCH PROTECTS THE PROPERTY OF THE DEAD

The Church had a duty to make sure that the property of the dead was divided according to their wishes. The goods of parish priests, apparently, were particularly vulnerable 'for the instinct of the malicious is, immediately after the death ... to invade his property, reap his corn, if it is in the ear, or pull up his root crops.'[1]

Wills and all matters concerned with the goods of the dead to be found in bishops' registers are generally of people who held property outside a single archdeaconry in the diocese (when the archdeacon would be responsible) but within a single diocese. The wills of prominent testators and of those with property in more than one diocese would pass to the Prerogative Court of Canterbury (hence PCC wills).

There are, disappointingly, few entire wills registered, but there are enough related entries such as a note that a will had been proved and executors had been appointed or discharged to offer researchers some useful steps in creating a family tree.

Wills and testamentary business in the Registers

Ap Aaron, Elizabeth, wife of Sir Thomas: will proved at Banwell, 31 October 1345; administration granted to husband, who had no estate in diocese; John Walsche stood bail (Ralph no. 1922).

---

[1] E.F. Jacob, 'The Archbishop's Testamentary Jurisdiction' in *Medieval Records of the Archbishops of Canterbury* (The Faith Press, 1962), 37.

Ballard, Joan, wife of John, of *Banwell*: probate and administration granted to John, executor, 31 December 1446 (Bekynton no. 248).

Barkle, Maurice de, knight: will proved before Bishop Ralph 21 July 1347; administration to William de Hillesle, perpetual vicar of *Brympsfield*, and John de Cokkeshale, executors (Ralph no. 1996).

Barre, Lawrence de la: will proved 11 October 1336; administration to John, his brother (Ralph no. 1044).

Bele, Thomas, priest: will, in English. To be buried in parish church of *Portbury*; mother churches of Bath and Wells 4d; John Evans and Richard Hill of *Portbury*, husbandmen, reversion of his 3 tenements in 'Ballan' St, *Bristol* which Katherine Langley, his mother, had for life of his gift, the rents payable to the wardens of St Elyn's chapel, *Portbury*, for 30 masses for the souls of his father Thomas Bele, his mother Katherine, John Powke and Annys his wife, the testator, Henry Bele, and Anys, testator's sister; residue to his mother, executrix. Witnesses: James Godwyne, William Passour, Richard Heysell, John Lawrence, Thomas Russell, John Godwyne and others. 4 March 1525/6 (Wolsey, etc. no. 250).

Brunstill, Isabel, of *Banwell*: probate granted to John Walissh, executor; the other executor, John Henton, refused. No further account required as deceased's goods small. Banwell parish church 6 October 1446 (Bekynton no. 236).

Bustell, John, of *Banwell*: probate by bishop's commissary, administration to Joan, relict and John, son, executors. Chapel of Banwell manor 31 August 1448 (Bekynton no. 366).

Bytton, Sir John: will dated *Hanham*, 1313, proved Pucklechurch 1314 before Droxford: he wished to be buried in new Lady Chapel at *Keynsham* abbey; £20 for funeral rites; left large bequests to new Lady Chapel; to fabric of *Wells* cathedral and to *Bitton* church 6s 8d each; to vicar of *Bitton* for obsequies (memorial services) at various unnamed churches £20; Thomas de Berkley and to Thomas de Cherlton, archdeacon of *Wells*. His son John proved his age (so that he could inherit) before Droxford, the archdeacon of *Wells* and many knights at Pucklechurch 16 May 1314 (Droxford pp. 71–2).

Chapman, James (or **John**), of *Axbridge*: Richard Poytevyn of *Bruton* to administer, 12 February 1464/5 (Stillington & Fox p. xxi).

Clyvedone, John de, knight, lord of *Clevedon*: will dated 9 August 1335. To be buried in the chapel of Blessed Thomas the Martyr in the church of St Andrew, *Clevedon*. To the high altar of St Andrew a silk cope; to St Thomas' altar a pair of vestments and a silver chalice; to Thomas, perpetual vicar of *Clevedon*, a horse and its knightly harness to draw him to his burial or 20 marks at his choice; the rest of his ecclesiastical vestments with a chalice to St Peter's chapel in his manor of *Clevedon*; on the eve of his burial 20lbs of wax to make four torches and that four poor people to carry them be vested in russet; on the day of his burial 100lbs of wax to make five candles to surround his corpse, and 20 marks for the poor on that day; to Emeline, his wife half his silver vessels for life, the other half to his son Edmund, who to have the rest on her death; the residue to support two chaplains, John de Evesham and John de Uske, to celebrate in St Thomas' chapel for his soul. Executors. Emeline his wife and Edmund his heir, Roger Tertle, and Matthew, his (the testator's) son; John de Pauyle, knight, supervisor. Proved before John de Middeltone, rector of Shepton Beauchamp, the bishop's commissary, in the chamber of the manor of Sir Edmund de Clyvedon, 29 August 1335. Administration granted to lady Emeline, widow, Sir Edmund and Matthew, sons of the deceased. Power reserved to Roger Tertle. Present John de Uske and Robert Valde, clerk, no date (Ralph no. 1019).

Cogan, Thomas: Petronilla, his widow, complains against his executors, John de Cogan, rector of *Huntspill*, and William de St Clare, who withhold her widow's third. Rural Dean of *Axbridge* to induce compliance or to cite them to consistory court. September 1315 (Droxford p. 98).

Croseman, Thomas, son of Walter Croseman, late of *Blagdon*: died intestate; administration granted to William Preste of *Blagdon*, his stepfather, 19 August 1513 (King & Hadrian no. 1017).

Derby, John: will approved before the official of the archdeacon of Wells; proved before Bishop Ralph at Wiveliscombe, 11 February 1348; administration to John Derby, vicar of *Frome* (Ralph no. 2173).

Ekyn, John of *Banwell*, 'cordwaner': probate and administration to David Spenser, executor. John Garnesey, perpetual vicar of *Banwell*, executor, refused to act. When the bishop found how scanty were the goods he released executor from accounting, 12 January 1446/7 (Bekynton no. 250).

Frome, Thomas,[1] canon of *Wells* and vicar of St Cuthbert's, *Wells*. Will dated 2 August 1424: his soul to Almighty God, Blessed Mary and All Saints; body in nave of *Wells* cathedral; cathedral fabric 40s; St Cuthbert's fabric 20s; his missal for use at the high altar and another book, chained in the church, Bartholomew *de Casibus Consciencie*; his cousin Richard Cockys when of age 66s 8d; Richard's sister Maud Chelewortb, for her marriage, 20 marks with vessels and necessary utensils at discretion of executors; Richard's brother when of age 66s 8d; Richard's younger sister for marriage 66s 8d; John Estmere, chaplain, a book 'Parisiensem' in a small volume *De Viciis et Virtutibus*; Sir John Alampton a white book *De Meditacionibus Boneventure de Vita Christi* with other works included; Sir John Massedy a book called *Januensis super Euangelia Dominicalia per annum*, in four quires in one volume and also *Exposicionem* on readings for the dead according to the compilation of Richard the Hermit; Sir Walter Mone a book called *Orologium Divene Sapiencie*; Sir Geoffrey Laverstoke a book called *Stimulus Amoris* with the treatise *de Incendio Amoris* in the same; Master John Orum a book *De Revelacionis Sancte Brigitte*; Sir John Crede a book *De Meditacionibus Sancti Augustini et Sancti Bernardi* with other contents in the same; and to the same *Gracianum super Apocalypsum* with other contents; Sir John Fontell a *portiferium* with musical notation and text according to the Use of Sarum for his life and afterwards for disposal for the benefit of testator's soul; John Sammell 20s; Walter his cook

---
[1] Emden, *Oxford to 1500*, i. 730–1.

20s; Emeri his servant 13s 4d; George his servant 20s; Roger Towyn 10s; Henry, kitchen boy 3s 4d; at his funeral every canon and vicar choral present 6d, at morrow mass 4d and at place of burial 2d; each parochial chaplain at St Cuthbert's 12d and each clerk there 6d; to every chaplain in La Mountroy college, *Wells* 4d; to the common hall in the Vicar's Close 6s 8d; to the hospital of St John the Baptist, *Wells*, for repairs to the infirmary 20s; to the Friars Minor of *Bristol* 13s 4d; to the Austin Friars there 13s 4d; to the Carmelites there 6s 8d; to the Friars Preachers there 6s 8d; remainder to John Masseday and John Estmere, chaplains, executors, to be disposed for his soul and for the souls of his parents in pious uses, to whom for their labour 40s each; Master John Rowland to be supervisor and to have 20s and a piece of silver. Proved at Wookey before Bishop Bubwith 28 August 1424; executors discharged 24 September (Bubwith no. 1247).

Gerald, John, of *Bristol*: executor, Walter FitzAdam, to administer, 19 February 1464/5 (Stillington & Fox p. xxi).

Hebbes, John, of *Rode*, intestate: order to rural dean of *Frome* to sequestrate goods, 1 August. Administration to Thomas Hebbes, brother, and John White, rector of *Rode*, under supervision of John Gawter of *Beckington* 'if he will act', 6 August 1440 (Stafford no. 801).

Hill, Alice, of *Exford*: appointment of commission to hear the dispute over payment of death duties between John Hill, late her husband, and the rector of *Exford*, 10 February 1433 (Stafford no. 397).

Hulle, Edward, knight: if he dies in England to be buried as near as possible to his mother; if he dies before her, asks her to arrange for 100 masses for his soul, 20 of Blessed Trinity, 20 Holy Ghost, 20 Annunciation, 20 Holy Cross, 20 *Requiem*, and to offer 1d at every mass and 1d to a poor person; outer part of crimson velvet robe to *Enmore* church for a vestment for God, the Virgin Mary and St Michael, the church's patrons; 100s to chapel of the Virgin, *Cleeve*, according to mother's discretion; 33s 4d to chapel of St Mary of *Adscombe* for some memorial there according to his mother's discretion; asks mother to be gracious to his wife; wife to have all fur linings of his robes, and his mother to have the outer parts for use in divine services. Mother Eleanor Hulle, executrix. Dated 26 August 1452. Probate to executrix, granted in chapel in Banwell manor 15 January 1453/4 (Bekynton no. 815).

Hulle, Dame Eleanor: will 'written on paper with her own hand, in English, and produced to the bishop' by Richard Walshawe, gentleman, of *Cannington*. Burial in the quire of *Cannington* nunnery; to the same nunnery a pair of silver 'chaundelers,' a silver cross and a silver censer, the white damask altar apparel, and one of three chasubles of their choice; Father [Roger] Husewyfe[1] all her goods at *Cannington* not otherwise mentioned, for himself and her servants; 1000 masses; poor folk to continue to receive gifts for their lives; bedding to poor; her clothing and furs to poor religious; alms in little purses to be paid out while possible, 7d in worship of St Katherine, 7d to poor; Father Husewyfe large and small breviary and psalter, great cup Edward, blue Latin Bible; Sir John Fortesku her best gilt cup; Richard Walshawe silver pot. Executors: Sir John Fortesku, Sir Roger Husewyf, Richard Walshawe. Dated 14 October 1460. Proved before the bishop 2 January 1461. The bishop's commissary granted administration to Roger Huswyfe, executor, 27 January. Commission to the rector of *Enmore* and the vicar of *Cannington* to receive Huswyfe's oath for administration, 2 January 1460/1 (Bekynton nos. 1347–8).

Juyn, John, knight: will, in English, dated 21 January 1440. His soul to God and body to be buried 'in the newe chapel at *Radclif* of Our Lady at Bristowe'; to his wife household 'beddynges, hillynges, coffers' in halls, chambers and kitchen, except silver vessels and ornaments 'of stoor' of silver and gold, and of his chapel, but wife to have basin and laver, charger, 6 dishes and 6 saucers, all of silver, a dozen silver spoons, 2 roses, 2 silver salt cellars and a silver pot; Richard Kenne and testator's daughter Elizabeth, should they marry, £40; Margaret Denys for her marriage 5 marks; Joan Whiteman for her marriage 40s; John Cadbury scarlet gown with marten fur; best mass book, breviary with musical notation and best chalice, best silver

---

[1] *Ibid.* ii. 990.

cruets, silver-gilt paxbread, 2 silver candlesticks for his chapel, a pair of cloth-of-gold vestments 'under the which I took the order of knyghthood', a pair of black damask vestments and a pair of white 'tartaryn' vestments, all to be used in the chapel of Our Lady of *Readcliff*, in the chapel of St Katherine where he and his wife sat, should he lie there, 'for ever whil thay wol endure'; Roger Saundres, priest, his robes as justice – a cloak, hood furred in miniver and a gown all of deep blue to pray for his soul; residue to executors for his children and his soul, that is Richard Newton, chief justice of Common Pleas, John Hody, John Fortescu, John Seynlo, and Roge Lyvedod (or Lyvedon); John Cadbury to be rewarded by them for carrying out their decisions. Proved before Bishop Stafford in the chapter house of the Carmelites in London by licence of Robert, bishop of London, 23 April 1440, when Hody, Newton and Fortescu were commissioned; Seyntlo and Lyvedon commissioned in St Peter's, Westminster on 12 May. The whole sealed with the bishop's seal in his London inn 13 May. Executors released 1 July (Stafford no 794).

Lambrook, Master William:[1] intestate. Sir John Knocston, administrator of goods released after rendering account: 14 November 1440 (Stafford no 812).

Lincoln, Christina de, of *Bristol*: will read before Droxford at Claverton. Executors, her son a *Bristol* friar, named by leave of his Superior, and a *Bristol* merchant. 14 June 1328 (Droxford p. 285).

Ludelowe, William de, vicar of *Compton Bishop*: intestate; bishop's Official to act, 14 November 1332 (Ralph no. 484).

Lugwardyn, John, canon and succentor of *Wells*: Thomas, bishop of Tenos, chancellor of *Wells*, John Pykman, archdeacon of *Bath*, and Nicholas Dyssham, vicar of St Mary's, *Taunton*, to administer 18 March 1501/2 (King & Hadrian no. 398).

Maister, John, of *Taunton* deanery: intestate; administration granted 1322 (Droxford p. 208).

Marys, John, of *Banwell*: probate by bishop's commissary, administration to Joan, relict and executrix. Bishop exempted

---

[1] *Ibid.* ii. 1087.

her from accounting because of smallness of estate, Banwell parish church 7 October 1447 (Bekynton no. 298).

Mathew, John, chaplain, of *Wells*: Thomas Smyth of *Wells* to administer, 4 March 1464/5 (Stillington & Fox p. xxi).

Mayow, William, of *Banwell*: probate by bishop's commissary, administration to Agnes, relict and executrix. Exempted from accounting because of small estate. Banwell parish church 6 April 1448 (Bekynton no. 328).

Meriet, Sir John de: removed the heart from his wife's body in defiance of her expressed wishes (?in her will) and was excommunicated. He was absolved from his crime thanks to the pope's penitentiary but Bishop Droxford ordered him both to do penance and to bury her heart with her body. 1314 (Droxford p. 70).

Mohun, Ada de, wife of John de Mohun III. Her son Payn reported to Droxford that she had bequeathed him a cope ornamented with gold and relics but his father, as executor, had not delivered 50 marks which she had also bequeathed to Payn and three younger siblings. Bishop ordered executor to deliver, 13 March 1323/4 (Droxford p. 231).

Montacute, Sir William de: will dated *Bordeaux*, 1319; to be buried in church of St Peter and Paul, *Bruton*; houses in city of *London* to wife; to daughter Mary the *maritagium* of Richard, son and heir of Sir Thomas de Cogan, which he bought of the king; his moveable goods to his executors (widow, son, and chaplain, Walkelin) for funeral costs and for his soul's good. Witnesses: wife, Friar William de Calne, and his clerk William de Longley. Proved before Droxford at Wiveliscombe church 26 March 1320. Moveable goods sequestrated until widow and Walkelin arrived and obtained grant of administration. Walkelin, rector of *Chedzoy*, and Gilbert, rector of *Goathill*, given charge of goods in inventory until executors take out administration. Copy of inventory to be sent to bishop. 20 April, at instance of widow, Walkelin and Gilbert to have custody of all goods (Droxford pp. 143, 147).

Morman, William, of *Banwell*: will proved by authority of Bishop Bubwith in Banwell church 13 January 1413; executrix Joan, widow (Bubwith no. 388).

Mountague, John, of Slough, *Stoke St Gregory*: will [*text not given*] dated 8 March 1558/9 (Wolsey, etc. no. 936).

Ploknet, Lady H de: was buried at her request at *Sherborne* abbey; her son Sir Alan reburied her 'in a more humble place' and was excommunicated after defying the bishop, ?1315 (Droxford p. 88).

Wytham, Roger de, rector of *Donyatt*: administration granted, 1318 (Droxford p. 17).

Zonge, John le, of *Kingston Seymour*: administration granted to Miles, his son, and Alice, his widow, executors, 25 August 1335 (Ralph no. 930).

PART THREE:
RURAL AND URBAN LANDSCAPES

CHAPTER VIII
THE COUNTRYSIDE

By the beginning of the 14th century, when our registers begin, the population of Somerset was greater than ever before, worshipping in churches in over 500 parishes of varying sizes. By the beginning of the 15th century, after the devastation of the Black Death, a few communities had disappeared entirely but, almost in defiance of such a huge loss of population and economic collapse, new buildings and especially towers, are witness to much generosity and devotion. The bishops' registers tell very little of this story: mainly about what parishioners contributed to the income of rectors and vicars by way of tithes and offerings and what those clergy could in turn pay by way of taxes.

John Droxford, coming to his diocese at the beginning of the 14th century, took over, like all his fellow bishops, a piece of England already largely divided into parishes, each with its own church, formed before the Norman Conquest. Some of those churches, called minsters, originally served what by his time had come to be towns, and had established chapels in their large parishes to serve satellite settlements, traces of which remarkably survive, almost by accident in two registers (*see below*). Newer settlements might still develop, sometimes in cleared woodland (Woodwick), from moorland enclosure (Hawkridge and Withypool), or industrial exploitation (Coleford). When Droxford came, Somerset's population was larger than it had ever been, and farming was successful enough to support it. There followed the ravages of the Black Death, where the population fell, perhaps in places by as much as one half, and then followed a long and faltering recovery with frequent outbreaks of plague, problems summed up in the 15th century in one place as the 'prevailing mortality and scarcity of tenants' and in another as 'the prevailing mortality, the dearth of parishioners, and the other misfortunes of this present age' (Bekynton nos. 1527, 1627).

A countryside deprived of half its labour force, a community of half its members and a church of half its supporters in the 1350s faced nothing short of disaster. Yet the amazing number of churches rebuilt and increased in size after that time seems to suggest a kind of recovery, and it was the responsibility of successive bishops to ensure that the churches and chapels in this landscape were served properly, and their people followed the faith of their ancestors from birth to death.

Tithes and glebe

Rectors and vicars in the countryside depended for most of their income on the proceeds of farming: they held land in varying amounts, both ploughed and under grass (glebe), they were paid a tenth share (tithe) of many of the crops grown, animals and birds raised and other items produced by their parishioners, and they also collected offerings made in church in return for spiritual services such as weddings and funerals. Glebe and tithes listed when a bishop made arrangements for individual clergy to be paid provide a picture of farming in parishes right across the diocese.

'Small' tithes (produce of gardens and farmyards), offerings in church and tithe of mills were thought sufficient to support the first vicar of Evercreech in Bishop Jocelin's time (1206–42), leaving the rectors, the hospital of St John in Wells, with the tithes of grain, hay, wool, lambs and cheese (Bekynton no. 1527). Tithes of grain and hay and small tithes may be assumed everywhere, but at Wiveliscombe in 1262 the vicar had a tithe of the venison in the bishop's park (Droxford p. 170). At Winsford in 1281 wool, lambs, foals, calves, young pigs, geese, cheese, butter, flax, honey, mills and hay were listed (Bekynton no. 825); at Kingsbury Episcopi in 1302 lambs, calves, foals, geese, young pigs, doves, eggs, wool, flax, honey, cheese, milk, butter, apples and pears (Bekynton no. 296); at Stockland Bristol in 1317 swans, but not for the vicar; at Bathwick in 1321 wool, lambs and honey. In the same year at St Decumans butter, milk, wool, hay and doves; at Yatton in 1326 honey and grazing for two beasts and a horse (Droxford pp. 129, 180, 270). In Bishop Ralph's time, before the Black Death, Burnham produced lambs' wool, cheese and calves, Woolavington fruit and geese, Northover lambs and, unusually, ale, probably at the inns that lined the road running south into Ilchester. The new vicar of Meare in 1351 had no share in the abbot of Glastonbury's fish; but from 1362 the vicars of Creech received tithes of hay, wool, milk, mills, fisheries, '&c.' (Ralph nos. 1152, 1209, 1295, 2585, 96*).

The arrangement approved by Bishop Harewell for vicars of East Coker from 1385 suggests a parish of great variety, little affected by general agricultural depression, and included not only the usual wool but alders, woolfells, skins, chickens, geese, ducks, doves, eggs, milk and dairy produce, flax, hemp, thorns and coppice wood and even a yule log (Bubwith no. 882 (p. 367)). By the late 1420s, vicars under financial strain either asked the bishop to intervene (Castle Cary 1426, Shepton Montague 1430) or quarrelled with their parishioners for not paying what they owed (lambs at Combe St Nicholas in 1431, fish at Minehead in 1433) (Stafford, nos. 73, 292, 330, 422). Enquiries into poverty were ordered at Holcombe in 1433, Uphill and West Quantoxhead in 1434 (Stafford nos. 452, 480). Bishop Bekynton significantly increased vicars' incomes at Puriton in 1451 with more pasture; in 1453 at Winsford with more land; at Stockland in 1454 more land including a meadow which had once been a fishpool and tithes of named commodities such as reeds, rushes and apples, but still not swans. In 1463 at Evercreech the tithes of cheese of the whole parish and the tithes of wool and lambs that were evidently also kept across the parish; and in 1464 at St Decumans some land and the tithes of cheese and apples from the whole parish (Bekynton nos. 559–60, 820, 825, 1527, 1627).

Minsters

All these parishes, and many more, were places to be found in Domesday Book and are still to be found across the diocese of Bath & Wells. The names of a few of them, such as Bedminster and Pitminster give a clue (like Ilchester or Dorchester in the Roman world) to those large early parishes with a minster (from the Latin word for monastery) at its heart, where a group of clergymen served together and spread the Faith in surrounding settlements. The two accidental survivals in two of the registers mentioned above tell their own story clearly. The first, evidently found by some registry clerk about 1500 who thought it important enough to be preserved safely, was stitched to the edge of folio 201 of Droxford's register (Droxford p. 219). It describes the minster parish of Crewkerne at the end of the 13th century, when it included Misterton (meaning 'the minster settlement'), Wayford, Seaborough and Eastham.[1] A similar stray, on paper, stitched sideways to folio 30 of Bishop Bowet's register, reveals the minster based on what had then become Keynsham abbey, and included Keynsham, Queen Charlton, Publow, Filton, Brislington and Stockwood, and a chapel at Newyke or St Anne in the Woods (Giffard & Bowett no 159). A third minster, that of Taunton (by then centred on Taunton priory), was revealed in 1314 when the original parish included the two Taunton chapels, St Mary's and St James's, Trull, Wilton, Bishop's Hull, Staplegrove, Ruishton and Stoke St Mary (Droxford p. 69).

'Lost' villages and parishes

Large parishes like those were interspersed with much smaller, single ones, some so small that during the later Middle Ages they became what used to be called 'lost' villages, places once large enough to have their own churches or chapels but which had, perhaps even then, become no more than humps and hollows in fields. One such 'lost' place was Hawkwell, a place large enough to be mentioned in Domesday Book and somewhere close to Dulverton, but whose last rector was appointed in 1327 (Droxford p. 267). Another, evidently on the outskirts of Frome,

---

[1] *Somerset Archaeology and Natural History*, 120 (1976), 63–4.

was known as Fairoak or Egforton. Bishop Ralph put John de London in charge of the parish in 1348 (Ralph no. 2178) and Bishop Stafford appointed three men in succession as rectors in 1429, 1431 and 1436 (Stafford nos. 244, 321, 576), but in 1446 Bishop Bekynton was asked, since the income was so small and 'the church is generally destitute of divine service and the cure of souls neglected', whether the parish might be united with its neighbour Berkley, the two churches only a mile apart. The long legal process, which spoke of the poverty of both and the small number of parishioners, was completed in 1460 when Fairoak lost the name and rights of a parish and it and its church were quietly forgotten (Bekynton nos. 1230, 1529).

A third such 'lost' place was Woodwick, joined in 1448 with its neighbour Freshford, on the edge of the diocese south of Bath, because both were too poor to support two clergymen (Bekynton nos. 44, 1566–7). A fourth union, only a mile or two away, somehow escaped being entered into Bishop Stafford's register and proved a little more complicated because the poor parish, Rowley or Wittenham, lay across the Avon in Salisbury diocese while its more prosperous neighbour, Farleigh Hungerford, was in Bath & Wells. The legal business, recorded among the records of the Hungerford family, tried to ensure that Rowley church should not be forgotten, that it should be maintained by its remaining parishioners and the rector together, and that services should be held in it three times a year.[1] No trace of the church now survives.

Other unions suggested in face of poverty proved not permanent. Standerwick was united with Frome between 1429 and 1436, had its own rectors in 1443 and 1453, but in 1454 it was said to have no parishioners and its church 'utterly destroyed' (Stafford nos. 225, 585, 922; Bekynton nos. 800, 897). A plan to join Capland to Beercrocombe did not come about in 1419 although its church was 'ill-built', there was no house for the rector and only two paupers living in the parish (Bubwith no. 913). Rectors were appointed in 1437, 1445 and 1494 (Stafford

---

[1] J.E. Jackson, *A Guide to Farleigh Hungerford* (London and Chippenham, 1879), 78–87.

no. 624; Bekynton no. 81; Stillington & Fox no. 1153) because land there still produced an income even if there were no people to be cared for.

Poor churches were not unusual across the country in the 15th century, the reason thought in 1415 to be either wars or floods (Bubwith no. 623), though more likely a general decline in returns from farming. At least 18 were excused paying taxes in 1431 (Stafford no. 392), including Sutton Bingham where in 1454 all the parishioners had disappeared, justifying the bishop in allowing the young rector to live elsewhere (Bekynton no. 775). A tax in 1445 found ten clerical payers on or under what would be now the minimum wage including the rector of Egforton assessed at 13s 4d a year, the vicar of Cloford 33s 4d, the rector of Pylle 40s, the rectors of Hardington and Holcombe 53s 4d (Bekynton no. 108). Between 1421 and the end of the century clergymen (usually vicars) in at least 28 parishes other than those already mentioned found their incomes seriously reduced and managed to re-negotiate their financial packages, including the vicar of Evercreech in 1463 and the vicar of St Decumans in 1464 (Bekynton nos. 1527, 1627). Others, like the rector of Capland in 1494, had enough influence to combine his poor living with, in his case, the rectory of Hinton St George and the vicarage of Chard (Stillington & Fox no. 1153). The new rector of Goose Bradon in 1522 had no parishioners to care for (Wolsey, etc. no. 111).

Problems and Possibilities

One other suggestion of farming problems was that parishes applied to bishops to change the dates of their annual dedication feasts. The people of Wookey in 1439, of Combe St Nicholas in 1440, of Kingsdon in 1461, of Shapwick in 1464 and of Norton sub Hamdon in 1501 all wanted the change because their feasts came at the time of the grain harvest or other Autumn labours (Stafford nos. 753, 800; Bekynton nos. 1378, 1613; King & Hadrian no. 318). West Monkton (1445) and Kingstone (1450) preferred October, too, perhaps for the same reason (Bekynton nos. 155, 528), suggesting the beginnings of Harvest Home celebrations.

Yet, there are signs in the registers of growing and prospering places, too. The people of Churchill, a chapelry in the minster parish of Wrington, were able to pay their chaplain to say daily mass there with Bishop Bubwith's permission in 1419 (Bubwith no. 827); in the similar minster parish of Keynsham, the people of Chewton Keynsham supported their own chaplain from 1460 in their chapel of Holy Cross, and those of Filton in 1527 persuaded the abbot of Keynsham to allow them to bury their dead in their own burial ground (Wolsey, etc. no. 472). Stoke St Michael in Doulting first acquired burial rights in 1438 and then the right to hold their own services in 1513; Chillington, in South Petherton, its own burial ground in 1494; Coleford, in Kilmersdon parish, its own chapel services in 1499; Stone, in East Pennard, masses in its chapel of St James (Bekynton nos. 673, 702; Stillington & Fox no. 1133; King & Hadrian nos. 22, 637, 1024).

CHAPTER IX
TOWNS AND TOWNSMEN

To be a bishop was to be a landowner as well as an ecclesiastical figure of importance, and to be bishop of Bath and Wells (in the middle rank of English bishops) was to be owner of an estate that included property in several Somerset towns. The registers were never considered to be a record of day-to-day estate administration, but there are enough references in them to give an idea of life in most Somerset towns in the Middle Ages.

Axbridge was never a large place, but in his will of 1348 Thomas de Dreycote, presumably of a family from nearby Draycott, described himself as a burgess of the town and referred to five clergy attached to the church, to a shop, and to the little fields on the moors below the town, one with a 'stokhous', on which the economy of the place largely depended (Ralph no. 92*).

William de Bode went to **Bath** for the bathing, so a jury declared, but he died in St Michael's parish there in 1322 as a result of his wife's ill-treatment. He was buried in the cemetery of the cathedral priory, but what happened to his wife is not recorded (Droxford p. 202). The bishops owned several properties in the city, and leases of several of them reveal something of the layout and the business of the city. In 1319 a lease recording that a parchment maker had held property in the market and North Street was witnessed by John the Baker, the mayor of the city. Leases in 1323–4 described a plot of land called 'Lotyate' near the north gate, a 'place' near the gaol, and four shops, two in Somer's street (Droxford pp. 131, 220). Among those people acting as guarantors for the satisfactory behaviour of the bishop's new gaoler there in 1344 were Alexander and Robert, dyers, and

Robert, a vintner (Ralph nos. 1526–7). Less than a century later, Bath's citizens, growing economically independent and wanting to exercise some political power, were in dispute with the prior of Bath over precedence – whether the bells and 'clock' of St Mary Stalls (the prior's church) should govern the timing of the bells in the city's other parish churches. The dispute, begun by 1408, resumed in 1417 and was finally settled by Bishop Bubwith in 1424 in favour of the citizens[1] (Bubwith no. 1266). Bishop Bekynton reacted in 1449 to the behaviour of Bath people who removed the clothing of the bathers and fined them for their modesty by ordering all local clergy to threaten perpetrators with excommunication and to order all bathers who had reached puberty to wear suitable clothing. The city's last appearance was in 1450 in a lease of a plot in Northgate Street which had a lane leading to a mill on one side. The tenants were to attend to bishop's court in the city twice a year. William Hogekyns, the mayor of the city, was the first witness (Bekynton nos. 441, 537).

In 1462 Adam Hamelyn and Richard Clopton, stewards of the merchant-gild of **Bridgwater**, leaders of the town's government in that year, exercised their right as patrons to present a chaplain to the chantry of the Virgin Mary in the parish church (Bekynton no. 1458).

The southern suburb of **Bristol**, south of the river Avon, was part of the ancient minster parish of Bedminster within the diocese of Bath & Wells. It comprised the three, almost independent, chapelries of St Mary Redcliffe, St Thomas and Holy Cross, Temple, and was also home to the hospital of St John the Baptist (in Redcliffe) and an Augustinian friary (in Temple).[2] In 1320 Droxford over-rode the chapel wardens of Redcliffe, giving permission for workmen to enter their yard to repair water pipes serving the hospital (Droxford p. 145). Bishop Ralph, while at Abbot's Leigh in 1334, ratified a deed establishing a chantry in St Thomas's under the will of Richard of Welles, a Bristol burgess.

---

[1] *A North Somerset Miscellany*, ed. R.K. Bluhm (Bath & Camerton Archaeological Society, 1966), 31.

[2] M.C. Skeeters, *Community and Clergy: Bristol and the Reformation, c. 1530–c. 1570* (Clarendon Press, Oxford, 1993), xi.

Its endowment was of two hall-houses with shops under in Fullers' Street, its chaplains to be appointed by mayors of Bristol (Ralph nos. 652, 654; Stafford no. 318). The houses were described as 'decayed and ruinous' in 1451 (Bekynton no. 593). Temple Street was named in 1337 as the home of an ordinand (Ralph no. 1135). Priests of a second chantry in St Thomas', at the altar of St Nicholas, in 1409 were for the next seventy years appointed by the masters of the fraternity of the Assumption, based at the chapel on Bristol Bridge[1] (Bubwith nos. 169, 1089; Bekynton nos. 446, 505, 551, 1075). Five men from the area accused of holding Wycliffite opinions in 1499–1501 were a tucker, a weaver, a dyer, a bottle-maker and a nail-maker, indicating both the industrialisation of Bristol's southern suburb but also, in those involved in manufacturing processes could more easily talk to each other, rather than labourers working alone out of doors. John Faukeys, licensed to hold a grammar school in the city in 1463, was perhaps expected to discourage such ideas (Bekynton no. 1519). In 1494 Henry Vaughan, mayor, and the commonalty of Bristol exercised their rights to present Richard Colyns, an Oxford theology graduate,[2] to St John's hospital 'Redeclyfpytte', and within a few days he had become Master (Stillington & Fox nos. 1119–24).

Two young men from **Bruton**, beginning their careers as clergymen in the early 1320s, were named Richard le Teynturer and Walter le Deighar, those names reflecting the beginnings of the town as a cloth-producing centre at the edge of the Mendips (Droxford pp. 190, 234).

The bishops' interest in *Ilchester*, the ancient 'county town' of Somerset, was principally in the appointment of clergy to its churches and in the affairs of a hospital there known as Whitehall. The registers mention the churches of St Mary Major, St Mary Minor, St John, St Peter and St Michael at Bowe (so called after its position over the town's south gate). There was also a church of St Olave. Bishop King in 1502 decreed, at the request of the rector of St Mary Major (long ago joined with

---

[1] Ibid. xii.
[2] Emden, *Oxford to 1500*, i. 472.

St Peter), that his church should be united with St Mary Minor and St John (King & Hadrian no. 471). The last known rector of St Michael's (it had been described as 'poor' in 1433), was appointed in 1494 (Stafford no. 417; Stillington & Fox no. 1109). The once important gated and walled Roman town was in terminal decline.[1]

The little town still had the county gaol. It had been lost to Somerton (see below) for nearly a century, but in 1328 Bishop Droxford thought some clerks might be imprisoned there (Droxford p. 289).

Two entries relate to **Pensford**. Sir John Joyn or Juyn, a judge, built a chapel for the 'house of paupers' in the little town in Publow parish, and Bishop Stafford commissioned his suffragan to consecrate an altar for it in February 1435 (Stafford no. 506). Bishop Bekynton in 1448 found that the community, without his permission, had appointed a chaplain to serve their chapel without his authority and promptly put both the chaplain and the chapel under interdict. In defiance of that, Robert Tanner of Pensford had persuaded a Dominican friar from Gloucester, two monks of Bath and a secular chaplain whose name was not known to the bishop to say mass and hold other services there. Bekynton at first appointed two senior clergy to enquire and punish as necessary but on the same day, at the request of Sir James Ormond and 'in consideration of the approach of Christmas', lifted the interdict on the chapel so as not to deprive the people of Pensford of spiritual comfort (Bekynton nos. 381–3).

In 1308 or a little earlier a clerk named Robert de Oldelond was released from **Somerton** gaol. Regularly, the bishop demanded from the royal justices the release of accused clergymen from the gaol there so that they might be tried in the church's own courts. Bishop Droxford's register also contains four licences issued by him to the royal justices sitting in the county, allowing anyone acting as a witness to take an oath, even though the sessions were to be held in Lent (Droxford pp. 13, 28, 96, 121, 151, 179, 213).

---

[1] *History of Somerset (V.C.H.)*, iii, ed. R.W. Dunning (Oxford University Press, 1974), 196–9.

The people of *Taunton* had similarly demonstrated their independence in 1341 in being prepared, this time with the bishop's approval, to pay their own chaplain to take a service every morning for a year (Ralph no. 1648). By the early 1440s that independence had resulted in St Mary Magdalene's church having so many chantry priests and other clergy there that the conduct of services had become a shambles, though the archbishop of Canterbury's intervention had been ignored (Bekynton no. 59).

The bishop was obviously a significant presence in **Wells** and his property there was extensive. References to the city are, like those to Bath, curiously few, usually involving leases of property with their landmarks and the occupations of tenants. Thus in 1326 Alexander the barber took a house with the Guildhall on one side and the cathedral cemetery on the other (Droxford no. 21). Bishop Ralph registered the text of King Edward III's charter granted to the city in 1344, according to which the men of Wells acquired the same rights as those of Salisbury. There were also leases: a plot in Chamberlain Street, the lease witnessed by, among others, John the salter and John merchant in 1343; another in the street called 'Bizestewalle' in 1345; and another to John the smith of Southover of a site by the cemetery of the chapel of St Thomas there in 1345. 'Certain' houses of the canons were said in 1362 to be 'very ruinous and altogether derelict' (Ralph nos. 1528, 1753, 1927, 1929, *106).

John King, a Wells tailor, was a plaintiff in the bishop's court in 1424, and a city lease of 1456, for some unknown reason entered in Bekynton's register, involved another Wells tailor, William Chiew, and was witnessed by John Godewyn, 'master' of the city, and two constables. The property, in 'Cuthbertstrete', stretched back northwards to a ditch called 'Luteborn', and Chiew was to rebuild the house occupying it (Bubwith no. 1242; Bekynton no. 1013). A document dated 23 June 1459 completes[1] the story of Bekynton's generous grant of 'divers costly buildings' and their site on the north side of the market place to the dean and

---

[1] The gift of the site had been made in 1451: *[Calendar of the] Manuscripts of the Dean and Chapter of Wells* (Historical Manuscripts Commission, 1907, 1914), i. 435.

chapter of the cathedral by allowing gutters to be constructed to take water from St Andrew's well to the city's fountain. Among the notable buildings in the city were the great gate of St John's hospital and the 'sumptuously-adorned' house of the cathedral Precentor (Bekynton nos. 166, 844, 1220).

Hugh de la Burgh and other merchants of the borough of **Westover** (also known as Suthwyk or Frog Lane) complained to Bishop Droxford in 1321 that they had been charged toll and customs at fairs and markets contrary to a royal charter in favour of all Bishop Jocelin's tenants (Droxford p. 190). Westover had then only recently been laid out across the Parrett from Langport as a way of raising the value of the bishop's manor of Huish from rent-paying businessmen like Hugh. It remained a very small settlement, but its site can still be visited.[1]

A disastrous fire in **Yeovil** in 1450 caused Bishop Bekynton to offer an indulgence of forty days off purgatory to suitably contrite people prepared to offer help to sufferers. The fire, on Trinity Sunday, destroyed 117 houses, 26 of them belonging to two chantries (Holy Trinity and the Virgin Mary) inside the parish church, 11 to the chantry of the Virgin Mary outside the church, and 2 to the town's almshouse (Bekynton no. 519).

---

[1] *History of Somerset*, iii, ed. Dunning, 6.

CHAPTER X
THE BISHOPS' ESTATES

The estates of the bishops required their own administration, but decisions needing formal record found their way into the registers.

The bishops of Bath & Wells had estates stretching across Somerset from Wiveliscombe in the west to Claverton in the east, together with others at Pucklechurch and Westerleigh in Gloucestershire, Compton in Berkshire, Dogmersfield in Hampshire, and a house in London in the parish of St Clement Dane near Temple Bar. Bishops could not be expected to know much about estate management and agriculture, and naturally relied on others for advice, and their registers often include formal leases to tenants which are witnessed by a group of laymen with the knowledge and experience the bishop lacked. Thus, a lease of some property in Congresbury manor granted to his steward Sir John Randolf and his wife was witnessed in London by members of what might be called the bishop's council: Sir John and Sir Matthew de Clyvedon, Sir John de Sutton, Sir John de Beauchamp, Sir Stephen Delamore, Richard Rodney, William de Scoville, John Fitzpaine 'and others' (Droxford pp. 157–8). Bekynton's register, similarly, records a steward (who held manorial courts), a receiver-general, surveyors, auditors and bailiffs (Bekynton e.g. nos. 68, 70, 351, 1221, 1621).

Droxford evidently left the estates in poor shape and Ralph found himself seriously in debt for some time (Ralph nos. 121, 208, 2170). Together those estates placed the bishops seventh in order of wealth of the sixteen English bishops. Droxford also had properties at Walton on the Hill and Pirbright (Surrey) and

West Greenwich (Kent) to boost his income, Ralph had an estate at Oxstead (Surrey). Judging by the number of times they dated documents from their various houses, both Droxford and Ralph preferred to be at Wiveliscombe (a good place to hide during the Black Death); Bekynton liked Wookey and Banwell, King liked Banwell, Stillington was happier in London. None of them stayed at the Palace in Wells for long.

The registers contain irregular references to the appointments of estate stewards and receivers, auditors and some minor officers like parkers and bailiffs. The senior offices were usually held by local gentry like Sir John de Clyvedon, steward 1315–24, 1327–9; Sir Walter Rodney from 1334, John Stourton from 1436, John FitzJames from 1451, Amias Poulett from 1493. Those and others acted as witnesses to the relatively few leases that bishops thought worth copying into their registers; they were the men who no doubt advised bishops on how to be successful landowners.

Houses

Droxford and his staff called his home at Wiveliscombe the 'court house', and by Ralph's time, and probably before, it had a chapel and a room set aside for the registrar, as well as other rooms, for domestic rather than business use (Droxford p. 91; Ralph nos. 1634, 1892, 2003, 2550). At Wookey, Bubwith used a passage or gallery between the hall and the chapel for business, Stafford once used a 'low', that is a ground-floor, room as a registry, and a great chamber for other work (Bubwith no. 1191; Stafford nos. 212, 693). At Banwell there was a main chapel and a small oratory where Bekynton did business (Bekynton nos. 1286, 1396); at Blackford a hall (Ralph nos. 606, 692); and at Dogmersfield, in Hampshire, on the way to London, a cloister, a great and an upper chamber, with an outer gate incorporating a stable with room above (Stafford nos. 651, 786; Bekynton nos. 270, 765). In the house (inn) in London in 1329 an inventory of furniture mentioned a chapel, bakehouse, larder, kitchen and *hospicio* (in which were two pairs of wheels for the water gate) and 20 keys for all the doors and gates; a parlour and a garden were named in Bekynton's time, when leases of small properties around it – to a bookbinder, a tailor, a glover, a fuller and a cook – suggest that some of the original grounds were being incorporated into the surrounding urban landscape (Ralph no. 7; Bekynton nos. 119, 816-19, 831, 838, 853, 855, 857, 860).

The palace at Wells, the largest and most complex of the estate buildings, has direct references only to a prison called the 'Cowhous' (1439) and the 'new' oratory (1456) (Stafford no. 717; Bekynton no. 1732), though an ordination in 1483 was held in the chapel of St Mark, Bishop Burnell's great chapel there.[1] But, a century and a half earlier than that last event, in 1336, 'certain sons of perdition' not only attacked the clergy of the cathedral but also 'strangers in our palace of Wells', imprisoning and wounding them (Ralph no. 1040). Was that event, perhaps, the reason for the building of the gated wall around cathedral and palace permitted by a royal licence in 1340?[2] A second register entry in Ralph's time, addressed to William Cammel, 'keeper of his palace or court of Wells,' refers to 'crimes and transgressions' committed there in 1351 (Ralph no. 2540). The moat was evidently not formidable enough. Later references to the palace in the registers mention a house for the steward, stables and an orchard (Stafford no. 811; Bekynton no. 1305).

Farming, Flooding, Fishing
The few leases that describe small pieces of their estates the bishops let to tenants, together with a few other leases and incidental references to unneighbourly disputes and natural disasters offer only scattered glimpses of life in the medieval Somerset countryside. Droxford's register mentions deliberate breach of flood banks and other destruction in 1315-16 and 1326, part of the running battle between the bishop, the cathedral and the abbot of Glastonbury (Droxford pp. 96, 98-9, 117, 264-5, 278) and natural flooding, poor crops and cattle disease in 1317 (Droxford pp. 5, 168-9). There were disputes and agreements about grazing on Curry Moor (1310), a mill at Lower Weare

---

[1] *Ordination Lists*, no. 104.
[2] 'The Bishop's Palace, Wells', in *Somerset & Dorset Notes & Queries*, xxv, 52-5.

(1316), the duty to maintain the park fence at Westbury (1317) and commonage at Rodney Stoke and pasture on Mendip (1318) (Droxford pp. 7, 18, 33, 174). A new tenant on the manor of Blackford in Wedmore took on 2 acres of arable land one each in the manor's two open arable fields; and the bishop in 1311 announced to his bailiffs at Blackford, Westbury and Wookey that he had appointed his friend (*ami*) Roger de Hanon as their *gardien*. The editor of the register speculated that he was to teach better farming methods (Droxford pp. 67, 114).

In the 1330's Ralph suffered trespassers in his park and fishery at Dogmersfield, an attack on his staff at Buckland, and thefts from Cheddar, Axbridge, Kingsbury, Banwell, Congresbury, Yatton, Kingston Seymour, Westbury and Wells (Ralph nos. 428, 434, 464, 566, 573, 1436). Like most landowners, Ralph was careful of his rights, making sure that farmers paid him for letting their cattle feed on Yatton moor, granting a licence for a tenant to dig for coal at Pucklechurch, and ensuring his rights were maintained in Mendip Forest, where he was challenged for cutting timber in his wood at Cheddar (Ralph nos. 509, 540, 826, 837). No clues survive of any direct effect of the Black Death on the bishop's estates, but what he considered extortionate demands of labourers affected his and others' property at Hocton (wherever that was), Axbridge, Banwell, Compton (Bishop), Congregbury, Yatton, Cheddar and Winscombe (Ralph no. 2475). Economic distress no doubt emboldened Henry de Forde to steal deer and other game from the bishop's park at Claverton in 1352 and to challenge the bishop's right to wrecks on the coast of Winterstoke hundred (Ralph no. 2707, 2792).

Fish weirs on Chew manor (earlier mentioned in 1338) were let again in 1426, the tenant having the duty to help maintain the park fence at Westbury. Friendly co-operation with the prior of Bath in 1442 (bound up out of order) brought the remarkable proposal that to allow the prior's woodmen to have an easier journey from his wood at Bathford to Bath, he might build a bridge across the bishop's half of the Avon and create a way across his manor of Claverton. The same agreement was repeated in Bekynton's register in 1448 (Stafford no. 34; Bekynton no.

327). The bridge, if built, has not survived. There was, it is clear, less co-operation elsewhere, with disputes at Langeyo in Mark in 1414 and again in 1452 where the rights of the bishop's Blackford tenants to fish was roughly challenged (Bekynton no. 700). Leases appear regularly in the register in the 1460s, but thereafter hardly at all (Bekynton nos. 717, 777, 1295, 1513, 1526, 1536, 1623, 1637; Stillington & Fox no. 1067; Wolsey, etc. no. 187).

CHAPTER XI
CHURCH BUILDING

The registers tell us disappointingly little to answer the common question when a church was built or altered. For a welcome few there is a direct record of when one was consecrated (replacing an earlier one); for one or two more the suggestion of recent rebuilding. For the cathedral, similarly, the information is significant, though not very precise, in spite of the support given by Droxford, Ralph and Bekynton.

Parish and monastic churches, and chapels
Surviving churches across Somerset tell of church building from the time of the later Anglo-Saxon kings and especially the great surge of religious enthusiasm that followed the Norman Conquest. How involved the bishops of the time were individually involved in the process we shall never know, but by the time of Bishop William of Bitton I, the clergy rather than buildings were the main concern. Yet in his statutes of 1258, which Droxford clearly inherited, he laid down that the repair and maintenance of the chancel of every church was the responsibility of the rector or vicar, and that the parishioners should look after the rest of the church. He also insisted that parish churches, churchyards and chapels in remote areas should be dedicated, that each parish church should have a covered stone font, two candles on its altar, and specified holy vessels and service books.[1]

The first consecration of a complete church recorded was that of **Combe St Nicholas** on 9 August 1239 by the bishop of

---

[1] *Councils and Synods*, ed. F. Powicke and C.R. Cheney, ii. (Oxford, 1964), 586–626.

Waterford. It was included in Bishop Droxford's register probably because of a dispute about the vicar's income (Droxford p. 266). Droxford's first was **Burnham**, built 'from foundations', that is a complete re-build, and ready in October 1314 but not actually consecrated until August 1315, a date, the bishop reminded the parishioners, he had accurately recorded so that the feast of the dedication might be 'devoutly kept' (Droxford pp. 78, 115). Early the next year, perhaps in response to complaints of the people of **Emborough**, the rector of Chewton Mendip, who was responsible for its repair, was ordered to re-roof both the chapel and its bell-tower (Droxford p. 110). In 1317 alterations made at **Bleadon** involved a change in the position of the high altar (the name implying at least one other), and the rector was permitted to delay its dedication (Droxford p. 122). About the same time, possibly because so much building work had been going on and no doubt also to make sure his fees were paid, Droxford issued a general warning that undedicated churches were not to be used for services and were to be properly consecrated within a year, the responsible rectors to have their names recorded and to be fined if they failed (Droxford p. 127).

Rector (the abbot of Glastonbury) and vicar together asked Droxford to consecrate **Meare** church in honour of the Virgin, All Saints, and especially St Benignus in August 1323; but rebuilding the ruined church at **Wembdon** was evidently delayed because some of the parishioners refused to pay the necessary rate. The rural dean of Bridgwater was ordered in March 1325 to threaten defaulters (Droxford pp. 219, 257–8). Over the next three years, probably in 1328 to judge by the bishop's movements, the churches of **Kilve** and East or West **Quantoxhead** were also rebuilt or altered in some way and were consecrated by Droxford, though it was left to his successor to collect the fees (Ralph no. 114). Towards the monasteries Droxford was certainly generous: he cancelled the fines imposed on Bruton priory, accepting their word that their unnamed churches and chapels were not finished; and similarly forgave the community at Woodspring in 1317 for not having their church and high altar consecrated (Droxford p. 171). St Lawrence's, **Wick**, a chapel in Congresbury parish, was an inconvenient distance from the parish church for burials. The community had by 1326 rebuilt the chapel and Droxford agreed with their claim that the old one had been consecrated and so he performed the same rite on the new, promising to return to consecrate the churchyard, thus effectively creating a new parish of **Wick St Lawrence** (Droxford p. 251). Earlier in the same year the bishop was prepared to support the parishioners of **Weare** who were wanting to build a chapel to be dedicated to St Thomas the Martyr (Droxford p. 277).

Bishop Ralph's register records the consecrations of **Shapwick** in 1331 and **Henstridge** in 1332, the first on a new site in the new village, the second a complete rebuild with four altars. The chancel at **Lympsham** was being rebuilt later in 1332, and there were plans to consecrate a new building at **West Lydford** at Michaelmas 1333. Some work had been done at **Beercrocombe** in the early 1340s, but the high altar was not yet consecrated in December 1343. Something similar was done in St Cuthbert's, **Wells**, for the bishop permitted the high altar to be moved 'to better light and adorn' either the chancel or the altar (Ralph nos. 110, 296, 410, 475, 551, 1768, 2808).

Churches must have been rebuilt or extended in the years for which there are no registers, and the best evidence must be the many examples of the Perpendicular style across the diocese. A chapel dedicated to the Annunciation of the Virgin Mary was added to the little church of **Seaborough** by July 1415 (Bubwith no. 563) and a chapel of St Mary on the north side of the 'ancient' chapel of **Idstock** in Cannington parish in 1426 (Stafford no. 124). Much more significant in scale was the complete rebuilding of the church of the Augustinian canons of **Stavordale**, paid for by John Stourton and recorded because in 1443 Bishop Stafford commissioned his suffragan, John, titular bishop of Holar in Iceland, to consecrate nave, choir, chancel and burial ground. A chapel in St Mary Magdalene, **Taunton**, given by John Warre, was similarly recorded because of a commission to consecrate issued to the same bishop in 1437 (Stafford nos. 630, 646, 928).

Bekynton's register records similar commissions to consecrate the new parish church for **Farleigh Hungerford**, built in 1443 to replace the old one, which had become a private chapel within the expanded castle for Walter, Lord Hungerford; a new church

10 *The new village church at Farleigh Hungerford, replacing the original that became the castle chapel in 1443: photograph, Author*

and churchyard for the Franciscan friars of **Bridgwater** in 1445 (Bekynton, nos. 6, 89); and a burial ground at 'La Frary' chapel, the former lay brothers' chapel at **Witham**, which was to be provided with a font in 1459 in acknowledgement that a village community had been established there (Bekynton nos. 1199, 1211). There are also references to a new Lady Chapel at St Mary Redcliffe, **Bristol**, in 1440, a new chapel on the south side of **Croscombe** church in 1455 and a new altar of St Erasmus in St Cuthbert's, **Wells**, in 1458 (Bekynton nos. 794, 924, 1178).

A chapel of St Stephen and two altars in the nave of the church of the little priory at **Burtle**, were to be consecrated by the suffragan, Richard, bishop of Killala, soon after Bekynton's death (Stillington & Fox p. xxvi), and the remaining registers record that **Long Sutton** church was recently rebuilt in 1493 (Stillington and Fox no. 1060), that **Burrington** chapel had been 'lately rebuilt' but was not consecrated in 1498 (King & Hadrian no. 138), and that the chapel of St Saviour, **Puxton** (in Banwell parish) was consecrated on 8 December 1539 (perhaps after alterations to the nave after the tower began to lean)[1] (Wolsey etc. no. 584).

The Cathedral
The registers offer very little direct, but still extremely important, information about the general support provided by the bishops for the cathedral at **Wells**. Droxford and Ralph each were actively behind the building of the eastern end of the cathedral in the earlier part of the 14th century, and their interventions have provided historians of the building with some vital dates. Droxford's first recorded contribution was in 1315, the gift of the fees he would have received for permitting clergymen to be absent from their parishes. The money was to be paid either to the master of the cathedral fabric or for the 'work on the cathedral tower.' In the following year the dean and the precentor were each appointed to assist an aged rector provided they handed over any profits for the bell-tower work. Anyone else wanting to collect money in the diocese for good causes was reminded that gifts to the cathedral should come first. The second precise reference to the cathedral is to the appointment in 1319 of a priest to celebrate each year in memory of Bishop William of Bitton I, who had died in 1264. The man was to serve at the altar of the Lady Chapel, described as 'behind the [cathedral's] high altar' (Droxford pp. 16, 86, 95, 107, 114, 136, 141). The new Lady Chapel was thus ready for use, though perhaps not yet physically connected to the rest of the building.

At the end of his life, Droxford turned his attention to the 'new work' that was going on. In 1326 he offered an indulgence of 40 days to anyone who contributed, and in the following year levied a tax of one tenth on incomes of employed clergy, to be shared between that work and the campaign for Bishop William March to be ..made a saint, with the obvious idea that the shrine of a saint would attract pilgrim money (Droxford pp. 250, 273–4). The new work was either the extension of the Quire to join with the new Lady Chapel or the embellishment of the Lady Chapel itself.

---
[1] A. Foyle and N. Pevsner, *Somerset: North and Bristol* (Yale, 2011), 586.

Ralph's first direct contribution was permission in 1332 for Dean Godele 'to be absent as long as he shall be engaged about the fabric.' Tragically for progress, the dean died in the following year, having been responsible for what was described (as it must have appeared to outsiders) as 'the demolition' of the building. The bishop, however, gave his support to the dean's executors to continue spending the money the dean had collected for choir stalls and other building work as well as for the March fund. At the end of the same year the bishop evidently came to realise that holding fairs in the newly-beautified cathedral was unworthy, and he banned both fairs and other 'business' from the building and its yard, an order that had to be repeated three years later. The continuing needs of the cathedral fabric fund induced him to get the rector of Yeovilton to promise to donate 40 marks (£26 6s 8d) should he fail to repair his own church (Ralph no. 1069). In 1340 the misbehaving archdeacon of Bath was fined 100 marks (£66 13s 4d) as punishment, also to be paid to the fabric fund, but the archdeacon's appeal to the pope against sentence probably prevented the cathedral from profiting (Ralph nos. 440, 492, 582, 957, 1590, 1619, 1627, 1653).

Ralph's most significant contribution to the life of the cathedral was the housing of the vicars choral. His register reveals that in 1351 he arranged that some rents from his tenants at Congresbury should from that year be paid to the vicars then living in 'that dwelling-house there built for the same vicars to inhabit.' That was the building, described in a will of 1348 as 'the new building of the bishop of Bath.'[1] In the year after the Congresbury rents were handed over, a much larger gift of property in the bishop's manor of Wells in Wellesleigh, Dulcote and Easton was added (Ralph nos. 2615, 2681, 2810). Thereafter some bishops recorded when they assigned vicars accommodation there: in 1424 William Twe received from Bubwith 'the first chamber on the east side of the vicars' close there, counting from the entrance' (Bubwith no. 1227). Tracing each entry from then until the last in 1526 (Wolsey, etc. no. 254) would produce a substantial number of names.

---

[1] *Manuscripts of the Dean and Chapter of Wells*, i. 215.

Almost as soon as he came to Wells as bishop, Bekynton reminded people that collections for the fabric of the cathedral took precedence over any others, a reminder he issued at least twice more. He also soon discovered that the building was 'in need of very great repairs in its roof and elsewhere' but that the chapter had no proper funds to carry them out. His first direct contribution was in 1452 when he paid for a chapel on the south side of the presbytery in which his own tomb was built. In 1459 he enlarged the choristers' house and in 1460 paid for the Chain Gate, 'the fair, strong and safe way' between the Vicars' Hall and the Chapter House stairs (Bekynton nos. 14, 46, 554, 630, 632, 1140, 1210, 1281). The bishop's other gifts to the cathedral and its buildings are not recorded in his register, but some are easy to recognise because of the presence of his badge, a beacon and a barrel (tun).

The chapel of the Blessed Virgin by the Cloister, otherwise known as Bishop Stillington's chapel, was built between 1477 and 1488 on the site of an earlier Lady Chapel. It is said to have been the bishop's gift, but the surviving register is largely the record of his vicar-general and includes no trace of it, though the bishop was buried there in 1491 (Stillington & Fox p. xiv). A chapel dedicated to the Assumption of the Virgin and to St Katherine in Vicars' Close was consecrated in 1498 on the authority of Bishop Oliver King

11 *The 'rebus' or badge of Bishop Bekynton – a beacon and a barrel (tun) above a letter T – on the Bishop's Eye, Wells: reproduced from H.E. Reynolds, Wells Cathedral: its Foundation, Constitutional History and Statutes (1881)*

(King & Hadrian no. 62). The building of the two chantries in the cathedral nave, for Bubwith (died 1424) and Dr Hugh Sugar (1489) and the pulpit given by Bishop William Knyght (bishop 1540–47), all three remarkable additions to the cathedral, similarly is not recorded in the registers.

PART FOUR
THE WORLD BEYOND THE DIOCESE

CHAPTER XII
THE BISHOPS AND THE NATION

In most registers there are traces of national history; in some there are many, often depending how close the bishop was or had been to royal government. There are plenty of references to Parliament, to the granting and collecting of taxes, and to the reasons for which they were needed. There are also, in the letters from government, requests that the prayers of the faithful would support the king in invasions of Scotland and France, defend him from attack at home and abroad and even improve the weather. Ralph of Shrewsbury's register shows the immediate effect of the Black Death; those of the 15th century the effects of fighting in France and political turmoil at home.

War with Scotland

Bishop Droxford's time in Bath & Wells coincided closely with the eventful reign of King Edward II (1307–27). The bishop had been at the heart of the government's war machine under Edward I, must have known the new king well and the problems he faced from the Scots. In his desperate need for cash in 1319, the king asked for personal support (Droxford p. 135). Two other entries in the register suggest that the bishop had personal connections with two of the king's sisters. In 1316 he offered an indulgence to all who would pray for the soul of one of them, Elizabeth, countess of Holland and Essex, who had just died (Droxford p.

107).¹ In 1326 he paid his third known visit as bishop to the nunnery at Amesbury to preside over the consecration of 36 nuns. The invitation to such an important event probably came from the most influential nun there, Mary, another of the king's sisters (Droxford pp. 163, 180, 269).

As a landowner, Droxford was obliged to send two knights to Scotland in 1310 (Droxford p. 60), but there is no trace of any other money raised to send the huge army to fight Robert the Bruce (King Robert I of Scotland), the army that was crushed at Bannockburn in June 1314. There is no trace, either, of the summons to Convocation in the month after the defeat.² But letters in the register show Droxford travelling to York for the meeting of Parliament in early September by way of Weyhill (Hants), not far from his manor at Dogmersfield, Fotheringay (Northants), Molesworth (Cambs.), and Skelton (Yorks.) and returning via Micklefield (Yorks.), Temple Newsham (Yorks.) and Felmersham (Beds.) (Droxford pp. 74–83). Thereafter the king asked for money in 1315, 1316,³ 1317, 1319 and 1322, all with the excuse that the Scots were threatening to invade.⁴ A private letter of 1319, in French, from the king, admitted how risky was his projected expedition and how great the danger of failure (Droxford pp 4–6, 83–4, 133–5, 203).

All the bishops were summoned to London in October 1321 'upon these sad public events.' Droxford replied that he was 'on [the] borders of Devon, too weak for rapid journey' and could not be there. The events were presumably the sentence of exile passed in Parliament against the king's favourites, Sir Hugh le Despenser and his son. The clergy eventually met in December 1321 (a meeting to which Droxford sent two deputies because the notice was too short), and declared the sentence to be unlawful. The

---

¹ G.E.C., *Complete Peerage*, vi (ed. Vicary Gibbs, H.A. Doubleday, D. Warrand and Lord Howard de Walden, (London, 1926), 469. She was buried at Walden abbey, Essex.
² *Records of Convocation, iii, Canterbury 1313–1377*, ed. Gerald Bray (Woodbridge, 2005), 12–14.
³ Ibid. 23.
⁴ Ibid. 55.

king demanded to know Droxford's personal view, even though he had already protested against the sentence in Parliament. From that same meeting the archbishop of Canterbury asked Droxford and his fellow bishops to encourage 'all who should ensu[r]e the peace of the Kingdom by prayers, fastings, pilgrimage or processions' (Droxford pp. 193, 196, 199–200).

Droxford was certainly now the king's enemy, and Edward wrote to the pope asking for his removal. There is no trace of that in the register, not of any politics or taxation until 1325, when there is a letter addressed by the bishops in Parliament, criticising the queen, then in France, for her improper relationship with Roger de Mortimer, earl of March, as reported in Parliament by the elder Despenser. The events of the next few months, involving the return of the queen and Mortimer, the flight of the king, and the summary execution of both Despensers find no echoes in Droxford's register, but in April 1327 the bishop received a summons in the name of the young Edward III to Newcastle-upon-Tyne 'for the king's service against the Scots' (Droxford pp. 253. 267). The king was summoning the bishop's knights, of course, rather than the bishop himself.

In October 1334, in face of another Scots invasion (they had recovered from their heavy defeat at Halidon Hill in 1333), Edward III wrote from York asking for public prayers, and in the following June for more as he was setting out from Newcastle-upon-Tyne to confront the Scots again. In August 1336 he was off again, and in the following summer he was requesting yet more prayers and more money to 'reprimand' and 'restrain' them - careful, non-military words which clergy might better respond to with generosity (Ralph nos. 893, 902, 912, 1030, 1143, 1275). But Scotland was soon to be of much less interest to Edward III.

War with France

Droxford, as lord of Winterstoke hundred, part of the Bristol Channel coast, wrote a most diplomatic letter in 1319 to the duke of Brittany reporting that local people had arrested ten Bretons as trespassers, and suggesting that they should be disowned and left to their fate rather than that war should result (Droxford p. 135). Early in 1324 Archbishop Reynolds and several bishops, including Droxford, asked the pope to mediate 'to bring France to a truce, and so to a peaceful settlement, which the King of England desired' (Droxford p. 224), but an entry on the first flyleaf of the register is the pope's reply: that he had asked Edward to make terms but had received no answer, though he had heard of the French invasion of Gascony and of the resistance to it led by the king's brother, Edmund, earl of Kent, the Lieutenant of Aquitaine (Droxford p. 1). After successfully resisting Scottish threats at the beginning of his reign, Edward III asked for money in 1337 to 'restrain' the French king, Philip VI. Almost immediately after the king's request, the terms of Edward's 'offer' to Philip mentioned a joint crusade, an end to French support for Scotland, and proposals for marriage alliances. The terms were to be 'expounded' to the clergy and people in the cathedral at Wells on Wednesday 9 September to encourage generosity from the diocese (Ralph nos. 1275–6, 1278). The French rejection of the terms signalled the beginning of the Hundred Years War. Edward's immediate actions were to begin raising money, and to be ready for possible invasion by recruiting men and organising a system of beacons to prepare for attacks on the south coast. Bishop Ralph's property at Dogmersfield in Hampshire explains why such defence arrangements were registered (Ralph nos. 1279–82, 1291).

In February 1339 the fear of invasion had grown and, following the agreement of Parliament, each county was charged to raise troops. Bishop Ralph and four leading laymen were to 'expound' what had been agreed and to assemble a Somerset force of 35 men-at-arms, 140 other armed men and 160 archers for service within a month (Ralph no. 1433). From July 1337 the king had seized those priories closely connected with French religious houses (alien priories, they were called), including Stogursey in Somerset, Otterton in Devon, Hayling in Hampshire and Goldcliff in South Wales, which had the right to present clergy to parishes in the diocese. The bishop was ordered in 1339 to report on those parishes and on any alien clergy. Parishes involved then or for the duration of the war with France included Puriton, Woolavington and Nether Stowey (Goldcliff); Chewton

Mendip (Jumieges/Hayling) and Martock (Mont St Michel/ Otterton) (Ralph nos. 1455, 1498, 1502, 1671, 1895, 2016, 2168, 2287, 2401, 2509, 2525, 2645, 2757; Giffard & Bowett nos. 125, 218).

The pope sent two cardinals to negotiate peace in 1340 (Ralph nos. 1476, 1478), but how could the French take the English overtures seriously when Edward III, while ordering the bishop to organise prayers for him 'about to set out for the parts of France, and has thought fit to send another army to the parts of Scotland,' dates his official order from the Tower of London, the 12th of August in the 16th year of his reign in England and the 3rd in France [1342], and then asks for money? Another expedition was planned for March 1346 and the bishops were called to Parliament to produce yet more funds and the clergy were put under pressure to find ready cash in anticipation of what they had promised three years earlier and hoped to pay in easy stages. And to add to the moral pressure on the church the bishop received a letter setting out the king's case against the undoubted aggressor, Philip of Valois (Ralph nos. 1490, 1492, 1926, 1941, 1945). Five months later prayers and processions were required for the army, then landing at La Hogue, the king's writ followed immediately in Bishop Ralph's register by an account in French of its progress: the almost miraculous capture of Caen against overwhelming numbers and the taking of the Constable of France. The return home of the English admiral, the earl of Huntingdon, with 'a strong and dangerous malady,'[1] seems to make this account unique (Ralph no. 1959). From Caen the English army went on to its crushing victory at Crecy. More royal demands sent from Calais (curiously misplaced in the register) explained that the king's army in France was still under 'urgent necessity and danger' in December 1346 and might the next payment of taxes be again brought forward? The Bath & Wells clergy, meeting at St Mary's, Taunton, declined to pay earlier than they had promised (Ralph nos. 1565–7).

---

[1] See *Complete Peerage*, vi. 649 which quotes Froissart and makes no mention of illness.

The Black Death

In the middle of August 1348 Bishop Ralph formally warned his clergy and people of the plague that was approaching the country from the East and urged them to pray for the mercy of God. The bishop was safely settled in Wiveliscombe by the beginning of November, and the pandemic was clearly raging by the end of the year, forcing him (and no doubt his fellow bishops) to issue a general order permitting the dying, in the absence of a priest, to confess their sins to laymen, and in extreme circumstances to women (Ralph nos. 2043, 2051, 2130). The shortage of priests and other clergy is made clear from the numbers of vacancies in parishes and chantries that were filled with less than the normal formality: 8 in November, 31 in December, 42 each in January and February, 35 in March, 32 in April, 20 in May. Some places were affected more than once. The effects were obviously devastating and long-term. As early as June 1349 the government issued through sheriffs (recorded in the bishop's register} a warning to surviving labourers not to take advantage to demand higher wages, a demand enshrined later in the Statute of Labourers. In the north of the county where the bishop himself was a major landowner, local clergy were ordered in August 1350 to warn labourers to 'take care to reform their broken treaties with all the haste they can.' The archbishop of Canterbury demanded much the same thing from clergy (Ralph nos. 2297, 2473, 2475).

Almost unbelievably, Edward III's government seems to have proceeded with its military activities while people were dying in huge numbers. Prayers 'for the king, and those about to set out with him for the defence of the church and his kingdom' were requested in October 1348, and a month later the bishop was summoned to a Parliament to meet in January. In the event it was postponed until after Easter because of the plague, but the business was revealed in the bishop's excuse for not attending – negotiations at Calais with the count of Flanders. Prayers for peace and for the king were again asked for (Ralph nos. 2126–7, 2144, 2147, 2321).

The government, of course, continued to need money to support its war effort: the excuse used was 'the defence of the church and the kingdom' or its 'safety and defence'. The need in 1353 was 'urgent', but no collectors had been appointed (Ralph nos. 2733, 2752). The last summons to Parliament in the surviving register was dated March 1354, the last royal writ is of November 1366. There were certainly meetings of Parliament and Convocation and demands for money in the 'missing' years that included the campaign that ended in the victory at Poitiers.

A Nervous King
Bishop Henry Bowet came to Bath & Wells on the insistence of the new king, and Henry IV was present at his consecration (Giffard & Bowett no. 2). His service to the king's father, John of Gaunt, in opposition to the wishes of the deposed Richard II, won him both the see and the office of Treasurer of England; and later the archbishopric of York. Bowet evidently made sure that prayers for the king, for the realm and for peace were ordered across the diocese in 1401–2 and again in 1403; and taxes were levied for the defence of the realm and the church (Giffard & Bowett nos. 37, 39, 110, 127, 176).

A tax in 1410 was needed because of the king's 'great necessity … for divers and urgent matters concerning the state, defence and utility of the church and the realm' (Giffard & Bowett no. 376; Bubwith nos. 93, 118, 196). A demand for prayers in 1412 seems to have covered every problem faced by the Crown: 'for the peace and prosperity of the king and realm' and delivery from 'wars, seditions, mortalities, pestilences, murmurings and dissensions, as well as the darnel, tares and heresies.' Those who wrote those words were perhaps thinking of the revolts of Henry Hotspur and of Owen Glyndwr and the growing appearances of heresy across the country (Bubwith no. 363). There was, incidentally, no reference in Bowet's register to the political crisis the king faced in the revolt of Henry Percy, but Bishop Bubwith's encouragement of any who would support repairs to Battlefield chapel,[1] built to honour those who had fallen at the battle of Shrewsbury in 1403, shows where the bishop's sympathies lay (Bubwith no. 127).

---

[1] The printed calendar renders the name Hateleyfeld.

To France Again

There are glimpses, also, of growing problems between England and France. Bishop Bubwith offered indulgences to anyone prepared to support William and Ellen Braunston of London and Joan Fuller of Norwich diocese in their efforts to redeem Hugh and Robert Braunston in 1410 and Thomas Fuller in 1411 from their prisons in Harfleur and St Malo (Bubwith nos. 40, 244, 307). The call for prayers in 1412 included special ones for the king's son Thomas, duke of Clarence, setting out to recover Aquitaine. It was followed by preparations for a new invasion of France in 1415 and a realisation that the country might be open to counter-attack. A clerical home guard was therefore created, Bath & Wells having to recruit 900 men, 60 of them as men-at-arms, 830 with bows and arrows, 10 of them as light horsemen. A slightly smaller number (839) was formed for the next invasion of France in 1418 (Bubwith nos. 552, 555, 785).[1]

The victory at Agincourt on 25 October 1415, which Shakespeare noted was the feast of the (French-based) saints Crispin and Crispinian, was, so Archbishop Chichele was to declare for his province, to be remembered as the feast of the translation of the (clearly English) saint, John of Beverley (Bubwith no. 685). The success of the invasion in 1418 did not prevent the men of St Malo from arresting Robert Brent and requiring another intervention by the bishop (Bubwith no. 803). Requests in 1419 for prayers for success at the siege of Rouen and in 1421 for peace and for the king and queen, whose marriage might bring it about, were among much routine business in the register that included in 1417 and 1419 the appointment of new rectors of Chedzoy and Breane, presented by the agents of absent patrons, Thomas Montague, earl of Salisbury, then in France, and Richard Beauchamp, earl of Warwick, 'in parts beyond seas' (Bubwith nos. 723, 841, 868, 1038).

At home summonses to Parliament and Convocation and general orders from the archbishop of Canterbury revealed

---

[1] The original answers to the king in reply to his requests for men, sent from Wells by John Roland, the vicar-general and copied in the register, still survive in the National Archives as S.C. 1 57/52–3.

the general concerns of the government at home: the threat of Lollardy in 1413, with particular activities in London, Rochester and Hereford dioceses associated with the beliefs of Sir John Oldcastle; prayers for 'the serenity of the air' and against so much rain in 1414; for peace of the church and fine weather in 1415, 1416 and 1417 (Bubwith nos. 451, 455, 498, 547, 704). John, duke of Bedford, the king's brother, as guardian of England, called and postponed Parliament in 1415 and 1417 in the absence of the Henry V in France, but by 1420 his place as guardian had been taken by his youngest brother Humphrey, duke of Gloucester (Bubwith nos. 573, 577, 721, 932, 988). A rarely-recorded royal writ appointed one of the king's justices to hear a case at Crewkerne in July 1415 which established that William Bonville was patron of Buckland St Mary (Bubwith no. 562). Bonville's main opponent, Edward, duke of York, the king's uncle, was the most prominent casualty on the English side at Agincourt three months later.

Prayers for the king and queen and for peace in the kingdoms of France and England were requested in July 1421, but within little more than a year the king was dead. Bubwith's summons to Parliament a month later was issued in the name of the (9-month-old) king and council. The king, church and realm became the general objects of prayers and processions, and specifically the king's uncles, John, duke of Bedford, regent of France, and Humphrey, duke of Gloucester, protector and defender of England (Bubwith nos. 1038, 1133, 1188). That shared government arrangement lasted until Henry VI was crowned at Westminster in November 1429.[1]

Bishop John Stafford, a member of the royal council, was absent in France with the young king between March and September 1430 and Master David Price acted as vicar-general in his absence (Stafford, nos. 266, 278). Anne, countess of Huntingdon, acted as patron of West Lydford in 1431 when her husband was abroad (Stafford no. 302), fighting in northern

---

[1] *Handbook of British Chronology*, ed. E.B. Fryde, D.E. Greenway, S. Porter and I. Roy (Royal Historical Society, 1986), 41.

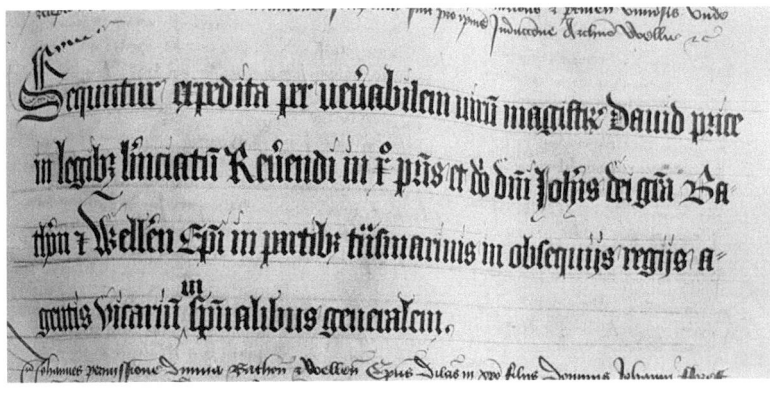

12 Master David Price becomes vicar-general when Bishop Stafford goes to France with the royal household in March 1430: S.H.C. D/D/B reg 5, f. 56

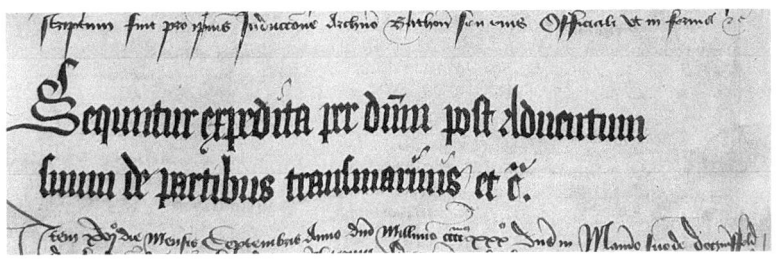

13 Bishop Stafford resumes business on his return from France in September 1430: S.H.C. D/D/B reg 5, f. 57

France.[1] The continuing war otherwise hardly touched the administration of the diocese except through the inevitable demand for more money, which produced lists of parishes not normally taxed but now liable, so great was the government's need, and others usually taxed whose value had fallen so much they were exempt (Stafford nos. 31, 344, 392, 420, 782).

Bishop Stafford in 1441 encouraged prayers from the faithful of his diocese for union among the churches, peace between rulers and for the good estate of their 'most Christian' king (Stafford no. 827). Bishop Bekynton's rule covered the years when the French war came to a disastrous end. Non-taxed benefices were

---

[1] *Complete Peerage*, v. 207.

charged again in 1445, 1447, 1449 and 1450. The 1449 grant including a charge of 6s. 8d. on every man paid to serve in a church, its schedule providing the names of several hundred men and their churches (Bekynton nos. 100, 267, 477–8, 486–8, 530). Processions and prayers were urgently ordered in 1452 'for the happy outcome of the expedition of the earl of Shrewsbury ... for the protection and defence of England' but there is no mention of Shrewsbury's defeat at Castillon in the following year. An echo, however, is the will of Sir Edward Hulle of Enmore, which the bishop proved at his chapel at Banwell in January 1454 (Bekynton nos. 701, 815). Hulle, the last English constable of Bordeaux, was captured after the battle when Shrewsbury fell and died soon after a huge ransom had apparently been demanded.[1] The king still needed money after the war came to an end, and tax schedules are found for 1463 and 1468 (Bekynton nos. 1520, 1522; Stillington & Fox no. 118).

The Wars of the Roses

The year 1455 saw the first battle of the Wars of the Roses at St Albans. The last paragraph in the oath taken by Nicholas St Loe as sheriff of Somerset and Dorset in 1456 (not included in the oath of the sheriff of Herefordshire in 1445),[2] speaks of 'manslaughtres, roboreis and other manyfold grievous offenses that ben doon dayly by such as name them self soudeuors': public disorder was becoming common (Bekynton no. 1019). Registered diocesan business took no notice of the political crises of the 1450s, but a royal writ issued after a court judgement at Wells dated 'Monday after St David the Bishop, 39 Henry VI' [i.e. 2 March 1461] (Bekynton no. 1366) was two days before the king was deposed; and the new king, Edward IV, five months later, seems personally to have signed a letter in English requesting the taxes granted by the first Convocation of his reign (Bekynton no. 1391). Processions around churches every Wednesday and

---

[1] J.C. Wedgwood, *History of Parliament, Commons* (H.M.S.O. 1936), 482.
[2] *Registrum Thome Spofford, Episcopi Herefordensis, A.D. MCCCCXXII–MCCCCXLVIII*, ed. A.T. Bannister (Canterbury & York Society, 1919), 291.

Friday with chanting of a litany 'for peace and tranquillity of the church and realm' were called for in November 1462 'and for the prosperity and success of King Edward and his men now setting out against their enemies' (Bekynton no. 1464) as the king faced the invasion of Queen Margaret in the north.[1]

Thomas Bekynton, who had been closely and personally associated with Henry VI,[2] was followed by Robert Stillington, for a few months Keeper of the Privy Seal under Henry but through Yorkist influence, and thereafter for some years a loyal servant of Edward IV. In April 1477 Stillington suspended his proposed visitation of Glastonbury abbey 'by reason of important business affecting the welfare of the realm and the Anglican church' (Stillington & Fox no. 393). The nefarious activities of George, duke of Clarence, the King's brother, unlawfully arresting a former servant at Keyford in Frome and being probably implicated in a rising not too far north of London[3] may have diverted the bishop's interest. He may even have been sympathetic towards the duke, for early in 1478 he was committed to the Tower and was fined heavily before his release. He was back in action at his house at Chiswick in June 1478 and was still there a year later, but there follows a gap in his register until August 1482 (Stillington & Fox p. xi, nos. 653, 670, 673).

Patrons of various livings over the past twenty years or so had noticeably involved prominent men actively involved in the turbulent politics of the time: the Hungerford family and Richard, duke of Gloucester, disputed the patronage of Farleigh Hungerford in 1468, the duke of Clarence appointed a man to be provost of Stoke sub Hamdon in 1469 and another to be rector of Saltford in 1476; the trustees of the late earl of Devon (executed at Bridgwater in 1469) presented to Farmborough in 1471; the young Edward, prince of Wales, duke of Cornwall and earl of Chester, to Curry Mallet and to Stoke college in 1472, and to Curry again in 1476; the marquess of Dorset, the queen's son, to Puckington in 1476, to Lymington chantry and to Sock Dennis

---

[1] C.L. Scofield, *The Life and Reign of King Edward IV*, i. 262.
[2] Judd, *Thomas Bekynton*.
[3] Scofield, ii. 186–91.

in 1478. Richard, earl of Warwick, the Kingmaker, induced the prior of Taunton to hand over the patronage of Lydeard St Lawrence to two of his associates in 1470.

The Tudors

National prayers were asked in 1484 for the defence of the king and the realm, for peace, and for the serenity of the air and the tranquillity of the people (Stillington & Fox nos. 118, 762); there followed the battle of Bosworth when Richard III was killed. The appointment of Master William Ellyott, one of the clerks of the new king's chancery, to Whitehall chapel, Ilchester, in November 1485 by Henry VII brought a servant of the new government to the diocese (Stillington & Fox no. 795). The new rector of Shepton Mallet in October 1485 was appointed by King Henry's great supporter William Herbert, earl of Huntingdon; and the new rector of Chedzoy in 1487 was Christopher Urswick, King Henry's almoner, presented by the king himself by reason of the minority of Edward, earl of Warwick, Clarence's son, a teenager and a prisoner in the Tower (Stillington & Fox nos. 102, 125, 193, 216, 231, 347, 361, 424, 426, 510, 629, 788, 865). So was the church in Somerset involved with the great men of the realm.

There seems to have been mutual distrust between Bishop Stillington and Henry VII. Stillington took shelter in Oxford for more than a year until the end of April 1488; he was at his house at Temple Bar in May and June,[1] but a month or two after at Windsor where, perhaps deliberately deprived of his official seal, he had to use that of the college of Our Lady and St George to appoint William Smyth as provost of Wells.[2] He was at St Paul's, London, in March 1489[3] but at Windsor again in April, where he was obliged to use his vicar-general's seal to appoint a new rector of Axbridge. He used the bishop of Exeter's seal in September;[4] effectively powerless, he spent the last months of his life at his manor at Dogmersfield (Stillington & Fox nos. 940, 944–5,

---

[1] British Library, Add. MS. 41503, ff. 4, 12v.
[2] *Manuscripts of the Dean and Chapter of Wells*, ii. 109.
[3] The National Archives, E 179/67/52.
[4] *Manuscripts of the Dean and Chapter of Wells*, ii. 116.

988). His vicar-general continued recording business almost as if nothing had happened.

No national business was registered in the time of Bishop Richard Fox (1492–4), although he was at the same time Keeper of the Privy Seal. Bishop Oliver King (1496–1503), recently the king's Secretary, had orders for public prayers for the king in 1498, for an enquiry into the possessions of Eton College in Stogursey and neighbourhood in 1502, for a tax 'for the defence of the faith against the Turks', for an enquiry into the possessions of Syon abbey in Yeovil and Martock, and records of a dozen or more papal permissions for clergy to hold more than one benefice (King & Hadrian nos. 110, 185, 417, 469). In the register kept for Cardinal Hadrian de Castello (bishop, 1504–17) there is an order from the Cardinal himself, sent from London, to induct a man to Blackford chapel in 1507 and a statement dated 1508, signed by an Italian, Polidore Vergil or Castellen, archdeacon of Wells, in person in the register, that he had appointed agents for all his business in the diocese. There are also a royal order to enquire into cases of illegitimacy in 1509 and 1510, summonses both to Parliament and Convocation in 1510 and 1512, and notification of taxes levied by Convocation in 1512 and 1513 (King & Hadrian nos. 754, 776–80, 784, 828, 858–9, 870, 955, 960, 972, 997).

Processions and prayers were ordered by the archbishop of Canterbury in 1513 'on behalf of the universal church and specially of the English church, and of the King and his army within and without the realm', suitable spiritual support for Henry VIII as he prepared to invade France. Convocation also offered money to pay for the expedition, and the royal order authorising collection was signed by Katherine 'queen and general regent', since the king was in Calais. A summons to Convocation 'with all befitting speed' was issued in 1514; more royal orders to enquire into bastardy, one later in the same year and answered in the next, three more in 1516; and yet another about a bigamist claiming to be a clergyman and thus exempt from civil law (King & Hadrian nos. 1001, 1033, 1044, 1068–9, 1112–3, 1125–9).

The registers of Wolsey, Clerke, Knyght and Bourne are much smaller and selective than earlier ones and contain much less from external authorities: a royal order of 1522 declaring that James Percevall had recovered the patronage of Exford; a meeting of Convocation summoned in 1523 without apparent reference to the archbishop of Canterbury; and Cardinal Wolsey as legate intervening in monastic elections in 1524. Demands for money through Convocation continued; and so did demands for public prayers: in 1532 for 'the good estate of the Anglican church and of King Henry VIII and the prosperity of his realm of England, and of the universal church of Christ, and of those fighting against the tyranny of the Turks' (Wolsey, etc. nos. 122, 144, 146, 178, 344, 416, 447).

There is a crucial gap in the record between 1534 (when the king's teenage illegitimate son Henry, duke of Richmond, presented a rector to Stoke sub Hamdon) and 1541 (when the new bishop, William Knyght, with the king's authority, appointed a vicar-general. The pope and the monasteries were no more in England and the Crown presented clergy, for instance, instead of Glastonbury abbey, to the livings of Moorlinch and West Monkton. The Crown now also enquired about clerical appointments and vacancies to ensure that it received the money formerly paid to the pope. But the Church still called for public prayers: for Christian princes fighting the Turks in 1542 and for 'resonable' temperate weather in 1543. The King himself intervened in 1544 because people had taken part 'verie slacklie' in the required processions and now provided them with 'certayne godlye prayers or suffragies in oure native Englishe tonge' which should be used not just 'for a month or two and afterwards slenderly considered as others, but to be earnestly set forth.' Those prayers, presumably, were called for in 1545 because 'the King has prepared such a puissant navy as has not been assembled within the memory of man' and was facing troubles in Scotland and France 'and in the ports of Boulogne' (Wolsey, etc. nos. 468, 481, 494, 498, 528, 530, 561, 583, 609).

The death of Henry VIII in 1547 was followed by a Parliament in the name of his young son Edward VI and a mandate from Archbishop Cranmer for a royal visitation of the five southwestern dioceses (Wolsey, etc. nos. 661–3). Letters patent from Edward VI founding a grammar school in Bath curiously found a place among rather later business in the register of Bishop Bourne (1554–9), which was almost entirely concerned with the appointment of clergy acceptable to the Catholic regime in place of many who had been removed. The exceptions are a mandate from Cranmer's successor as archbishop, Cardinal Reginald Pole, authorising Bourne to make a visitation of the diocese on his behalf, and a grant by Philip and Mary, king and queen, to Sir Edward Hastings 'in consideration of his services against traitors' of the presentation to Creech St Michael, formerly the possession of Sir Thomas Wyatt, traitor (Wolsey, etc. nos. 827–9).

CHAPTER XIII
BISHOPS AND POPES

The registers of bishops Droxford and Ralph make abundantly clear that the popes in the 14th century were of great significance to the church in England, a significance that changed in character from the earlier 15th century and disappeared during the reign of Henry VIII. The Pope was the highest moral and legal authority, and his court (curia) provided decisions on appointments of clergy and legal disputes, so far as English kings were prepared to accept them. Thus, Bishop Droxford and his successors appointed (no doubt expensive) legal representatives to look after their interests at Rome and Avignon; and Bishop Ralph must have spent an enormous sum to secure the Pope's approval of his election as bishop (Ralph, pp. xix-xxii). For lay people a relaxing of rules might settle marital problems.

Taxation

Until the famous break with Rome in the reign of Henry VIII, successive popes extracted money from every diocese in various forms. There was, to start with, direct taxation, the oldest in the form of a small tax, worth only £11 5s from Bath & Wells, known as Peter's Pence (e.g. Droxford pp. 23–4, 69, 129, 228, 246, 257, 283, 297; Ralph no. 2814). Individual popes also demanded money for causes close to their hearts, and Pope Clement V (1305–14) levied a tax over six years for a crusade. This was understandably not popular in England and, recognising it could not be collected in full, his successor, John XXII (pope 1316–34), generously handed over any future proceeds to Edward II. The abbot of Glastonbury, collecting in the diocese on behalf of Bishop Droxford, declared he could raise no more and the bishop told the king's treasurer in 1317 that he had already sent 500 marks (£666 13s 4d), that authority to collect more had died with the pope in 1314, and that in any case bad harvests and cattle disease meant arrears could not be found. Similar reluctance was found by later tax collectors looking for support to cover the debts of Pope Benedict XII (pope 1335–42) and the expenses of papal ambassadors (*nuncios*) (Droxford pp. 5–6, 24, 76, 91; Ralph, e.g. 1002, 1065, 1123, 1243, 1609, 1707–8, 1766, 2470, 2498, 2527, 2689, 2693).

Among later direct taxes was Pope Eugenius IV's demand from all clergy in 1445 to raise troops to fight the Saracens. Henry VI, or perhaps his ministers, were not entirely sympathetic, but permitted the bishops to raise what they could. The result was a schedule of payments at the rate of 1d in the mark (13s 4d) ranging between Egforton at 1d and the Chapter of Wells at 44s 10¾d which gives a useful picture of the parishes and other livings of Bath & Wells at the time (Bekynton no. 106).

Appointments

Other demands from popes came in the form of foreign clergy to whom popes owed favours. Bishop Droxford and Abbot Fromond of Glastonbury resisted pressure from Pope John XXII to accept nominees, Droxford declaring that the pope's letter of nomination to the prebend of Ilton arrived too late, but found it worth recording that he spoke personally to the pope's nominee and wrote letters of apology to six other cardinals. The abbot said that the request was based on false information and simply could not be afforded (Droxford pp. 183, 209). No excuse was found to prevent Isuardus Gasqui from acquiring the prebend of Wiveliscombe in 1334 (Ralph nos. 679, 1979), and none for the three (and possibly four) cardinals who in succession held the rich archdeaconry of Wells from 1353, for another who held the archdeaconry of Bath in 1380, nor for two who were archdeacons of Taunton between 1383 and perhaps 1389, when the second became Pope Boniface IX. Four other cardinals laid claim to or acquired prebends in the cathedral.[1]

---

[1] Le Neve, *Fasti Ecclesiae Anglicanae 1300–1541, Bath & Wells*, ed. B. Jones (1964), 13, 15–16, 39, 49, 78–9.

Relaxing the rules

Popes also, for a consideration, often set aside clerical regulations, relaxed discipline, and permitted bishops to make appointments on their behalf or to offer spiritual benefits by means of documents which are variously described as bulls (from the Latin for the pope's lead seal, *bulla*), indulgences or indults, dispensations or simply papal letters. Thus, Philip Papiti of Florence, though under age and therefore not a priest, was dispensed to became rector of Merriott in 1313; and Thomas de l'Aleton, rector of Spaxton, was allowed in 1317 to leave it for a year to live instead on his other benefice at Heytesbury in Wiltshire, thanks to the influence of the dean of Salisbury, who happened also to be a cardinal (Droxford pp. 165, 175). At least seventy bulls from successive popes were noted in the registers between 1441 and 1511, most from the 1490s onwards, permitting clergymen to hold more than one parish. Among those so privileged was Dr Hugh Yng or Inge, vicar of Wellow, who appeared at Wells in November 1509 armed with two bulls from Pope Alexander VI and one from Pope Julius II allowing him to hold three parishes and two other sources of income (King & Hadrian nos. 852–3). Pope Julius appointed him bishop of Meath in 1512 and he was made archbishop of Dublin in 1523 and chancellor of Ireland in 1527.[1] Cardinal Wolsey, as legate of Pope Clement VII, issued similar licences for young men to be ordained in breach of the usual rules (Ordinations, nos. 252, 254–6, 258–61).

The Universal Church

Pope Clement V, who left Rome for Avignon and tried to organise a crusade, was also (with reluctance) responsible for the destruction of the Templars, the military order founded to protect the Temple in Jerusalem for the benefit of pilgrims. A consequence in Bath & Wells was that four members of their Templecombe preceptory were shut up in monasteries at Glastonbury, Montacute, Muchelney and Taunton to do 'penance' in 1311 and were still there in 1315; the one at Muchelney became a monk in 1319. A crusade had also been in the mind of William March,

---

[1] Emden, *Oxford to 1500*, ii. 1000–01.

bishop of Bath & Wells 1293–1302, and he had left 100 marks (£66 13s 4d) for the purpose. The bequest was still held at the cathedral in 1317 and a papal official threatened Droxford with severe punishment if it were not handed over immediately. Yet crusades were not popular in England, and the collectors for St Thomas's hospital at Acre were ordered not to permit alms to go to a preaching fund (Droxford pp. 43, 98, 129–30, 137, 261).

Occasional papal letters of a strictly religious nature included the establishment of the feasts of Corpus Christi in 1318 and of St Thomas de Cantilupe in 1322 (Droxford pp. 13, 208). Bishop Ralph in 1344 thought it necessary to have the text of a bull of Pope John XXII in favour of Carthusian monks, first issued in 1318, copied into his register by his scribe William Cammel, together with supportive writings. (The only two Carthusian monasteries in the country at the time were in the diocese at Hinton and Witham). Pope Clement VI (pope, 1342–52) in 1348 confirmed Ralph's order of 1335 that the cathedral chancellor should give lectures in theology or canon law at Wells between October and July each year (Ralph nos. 1294, 1780–9, 2402).

But international politics took up more space in the registers. In 1327 John XXII asked for the support of the English bishops against Louis or Lewis of Bavaria, Holy Roman Emperor, who set up a rival pope, Nicholas V, in Rome, 1328–30, and continued to oppose Clement VI at Avignon until his death in 1347 (Droxford p. 274; Ralph no. 1860). From 1378 until 1417 there were two, and for a while three, popes, a scandal that overshadowed the Church. By 1408 the supporters of rival popes came together at Pisa (a necessary though poorly-paid tax supported the English delegates) (Giffard & Bowett nos. 343, 355, 358–61, 372–3; Bubwith nos. 93–4, 102–3, 117–19, 121, 179, 623, 635), where Pope Gregory XII and anti-pope Benedict XIII were deposed in 1409, though Gregory did not resign until after John XXIII had been deposed in 1415. A second Council was convened at Constance in 1414 where Bishop Bubwith was part of the English delegation and a new register was begun by his vicar-general, John Roland, to record all his actions while the bishop was away 'attending the holy general council … for bringing about the union and reformation of the Church militant' (Bubwith nos. 515, 519).

14 John Roland begins his duties as vicar-general when Bishop Bubwith attends the Council of Constance, 1414: S.H.C. D/D/B reg 4, f. 88. The later registry clerk is at work again.

All faithful Church members were asked in March 1416 to pray at Wednesday and Friday processions 'for the peace of the church, for the king and for fine weather' and were offered 40 days indulgence as a reward. Further prayers for unity and for the Emperor Sigismund, a leading reformer at Constance, were ordered in August. Martin V was appointed the only pope and Bubwith returned from the Council in August 1418 armed with his authority to make reforms. The only bull from Pope Martin copied into Bubwith's register was one of 1417 allowing him to appoint ten lawyers known as notaries public (Bubwith p. xxxvi, nos. 547, 645, 1268).

Bishop Stafford, like his fellow bishops, was summoned to a Council at Basel in 1431 but appointed substitutes 'fearing justly the dangers of the ways and perils of the sea and being engaged in various and important business and service of the king' – he was appointed Lord Chancellor in the following year. He appointed new substitutes in 1435 (Stafford nos. 346, 542).

The council suspended Eugenius IV in 1438 and deposed him in 1439, but he was recognised in England and asked for money from the clergy to fight the Saracens (see above). Pope Innocent VIII (pope, 1484–92) expressed his support for Henry VII and Queen Elizabeth in 1486, and a summary of his letter in English was entered into Bishop Stillington's register at the request of the archbishop of Canterbury in 1490 (Stillington & Fox no. 971). Close co-operation between pope and king brought the Italian Cardinal Hadrian de Castello, official collector of papal taxes, to be bishop of Bath & Wells in 1504, to be followed on his removal in 1518, by Thomas Wolsey, already archbishop of York, cardinal, legate and Lord Chancellor. The break with Rome, begun with Wolsey's death in 1529, was temporarily healed in 1554, and the bull from Pope Julius III (pope, 1550–5) welcoming the return of England to the Catholic church, was copied into Bishop Bourne's register (Wolsey, etc. nos. 827–8).

AFTERWORD

The registers of fifteen bishops of Bath & Wells, beginning in 1264 and ending in 1559, were published by the Somerset Record Society between 1899 and 1940. In many ways it was a pioneering achievement, the most complete for any diocese, though Hereford runs it a close second, involving twenty-one bishops between 1275 and 1539. Successive editors of the Somerset volumes treated the texts in different ways, and introduced each volume as fashion dictated at the time. This guide is an attempt at a general analysis for them together. At the same time, it serves to demonstrate how the registers (as do those of most bishops) reach well beyond the confines of church administration to national and international history, and occasionally provide unique and unexpected glimpses for the political, local and family historian.

APPENDICES

APPENDIX I
NAMES OF MEMBERS OF
RELIGIOUS COMMUNITIES

Names of members of abbeys, priories and hospitals at elections and visitations recorded in registers:

Athelney abbey: 1458 (Bekynton no 1648); 1485 (Stillington & Fox no. 909)
Barlinch priory: 1457 (Bekynton no. 1646); 1488 (Stillington & Fox no. 998); 1492 (King & Hadrian no. 1168); 1524 (Wolsey, etc. no. 474)
Bath cathedral priory: 1411 (Bubwith no. 1271);
Bridgwater hospital: 1449, 1457 (Bekynton, nos. 1641, 1647); 1524 (Wolsey, etc. no 475)
Bruton priory, later abbey: 1448 (Bekynton no. 1649);
Cannington priory: 1351 (Ralph no. 2629)
Dunster priory: 1411 (Bubwith no. 1271); 1447 (Bekynton no. 1639); 1525 (Wolsey, etc. no. 477)
Glastonbury abbey: 1456 (Bekynton nos. 1644-5); 1525 (Wolsey, etc. no. 475)
Muchelney abbey: 1463 (Bekynton no. 1650)
Taunton priory: 1339 (Ralph no. 1332); 1413 (Bubwith no. 1272)
Woodspring priory: 1458 (Bekynton no. 1649); 1525 (Wolsey, etc. no. 478)
Wells hospital: 1439 (Stafford, no. 725); 1462 (Bekynton no. 650)

APPENDIX II
CHARITIES AT HOME AND ABROAD

Bishops responded to requests for support for a wide range of good causes, covering personal distress, public projects and religious institutions in England and abroad, but principally and naturally in their own dioceses. Their response (and hence the information in the registers) was generally to encourage giving by the grant of indulgences.

PLACES

Athelney: abbey church ruinous, 1321: Droxford p. 189.
Bath: bridge and causeways, 1452: Bekynton no. 629.
    cathedral priory church fabric, 1310: Droxford pp. 60, 241.
    hospital of Holy Cross and St Mary Magdalene, 1332: Ralph no. 401.
Battlefield, Salop: chapel of St Mary Magdalene, 1409: Bubwith no. 127.
Bleadney: causeway repair, 1412: Bubwith no. 362.
Bridgwater: causeway to Poldens repair, 1325: Droxford p. 259.
Bristol: hospital of St Katherine, 1455: Bekynton no. 905.
    ornaments or bequests to St Augustine's abbey church, or pray for Montague family, 1329: Ralph no. 22.
    road between Bowbrigge and Dundry, 1445: Bekynton no. 132.
Crewkerne: hermitage of St Edmund in or chapel of St Reyne near, 1444: Bekynton no. 60.
Exeter, Devon: St Nicholas priory, tower, 1321, 1324: Droxford pp. 198, 242.

Glastonbury: ruinous chapel of St Katherine, 1476: Stillington & Fox no. 640.
Hatch Beauchamp: theft of two chalices, 1462: Bekynton no. 1419.
Hounslow, Mdx: Trinitarian friars, 1466: Stillington & Fox no. 30.
Kenn: chapel of Our Lady, and prayers for the 'weal and tranquillity of the realm', 1457: Bekynton no. 1032.
Keneley, Worcester diocese (? Kenley, Salop): free chapel 'very ruinous', 1414: Bubwith no. 496.
Kingsteignton, Devon: 'Teynbrygg' bridge, 1422: Bubwith no. 1134.
Langport: Broadbow bridge, damaged by flood, 1472: Stillington & Fox no. 538.
hospital (leper) of St Mary Magdalen, 1311, 1337, 1452: Droxford p. 37; Ralph no. 1122; Bekynton no. 704.
Little Malvern, Worcs: collapse of bell-tower of priory, destroying part of church and chancel, 1479: Stillington & Fox no. 665.
Liverpool, Lancs: chapel of St Mary, to be built in the churchyard of 'the chapel of Seynt Mary of the Keye', 1452: Bekynton no. 735.
London: hospital of St Thomas of Acon, 1323, 1326: Droxford pp. 220-1, 261.
Old Cleeve: pilgrimage chapel destroyed by 'abundance of rains and fierce flood,' 1452: Bekynton no. 648.
Pontefract, Yorks: new works on chapel near, as memorial to Thomas, earl of Lancaster, 1331: Ralph no. 322.
Rochester, Kent: bridge, 1311: Droxford p. 43.
Rome: hospital of the Holy Spirit in Saxia, 1320, 1321: Droxford pp. 141, 192.
South Cadbury: hermitage or chapel of St Thomas the Martyr, 1411: Bubwith no. 291
Stavordale: priory, 1403, 1409, 1452: Giffard & Bowett no. 129, Bubwith no. 134, Bekynton no. 667.
Taunton: hospital of St Margaret, outside, 1418, 1472: Bubwith no. 810; Stillington & Fox no. 546.

Watchet: harbour 'well-nigh demolished and utterly destroyed' by storm, 1456: Bekynton no.1140.
Weare: building chapel of St Thomas the Martyr, 1326: Droxford p. 277.
Yeovil: 117 houses destroyed by fire, 1450: Bekynton no. 519.

PEOPLE

Braunston, William de, and Ellen his wife: ransom (20 marks needed) of their sons Hugh and Robert, imprisoned at Harfleur, 1410: Bubwith nos. 40, 244.
Brent, Robert: £40 to ransom, imprisoned in Spain or elsewhere, 1412: Bubwith no. 381.
ransom, taken at sea and imprisoned at St Malo, 1418: Bubwith no. 806.
Frenssh, David: ex-soldier, begging after years in France including held to ransom, 1450: Bekynton no. 547.
Fuller, Joan: ransom of Thomas Fuller of Somerby, imprisoned in St Malo, 1411: Bubwith no. 307.
Molyneus, Robert: huge ransom pledges after taken prisoner fighting for king of Hungary and prince of Moureyt, 1448: Bekynton no. 316.
Mottu or **Motton**, William, a Southampton merchant, trading to Aquitaine: ransomed for £60 (out of £100) from imprisonment in Bayeux, date unknown: Bekynton no. 358.
Person, John, the younger, of Winchester: imprisoned in Bayeux as surety for Mottu and facing prison again as Mottu is dead, 1448: Bekynton no. 358.
Pole *de Albo Castro*, Sir John, Count Palatine: ransom from prison in Constantinople of himself, his mother, brothers and sisters, 1503: King & Hadrian no. 507.
Sthaurachii, Sir John, a noble of Constantinople: for himself and ransom of his mother and sisters after fall of city, 1459: Bekynton no. 1254.
Walssh, Thomas: ex-soldier, begging after years in France including held to ransom, 1450: Bekynton no. 547.
Wittecomb, William, of Draycott: loss of home and possessions by fire, 1460 (Bekynton no. 1336.

APPENDIX III
ORATORIES AND CHAPELS[1]

Licences were granted to the following for divine service (masses) to be celebrated in chapels, chantries or oratories or as otherwise stated and recorded in the registers:

Alampton, John, perpetual vicar in Wells cathedral: oratory in his house because of his great age, in low voice, during pleasure, Dec 1430: Stafford no. 297.

Apperleigh, John de: oratory at *Appley* in *Stawley* with fit chaplain, Jan 1342, 1 year: Ralph no. 1696.

Arthur, Cecily, widow of William, esquire, for self and household: chapel of oratory in her house in *Bedminster* by suitable chaplain during bishop's pleasure, provided no prejudice to others, Dec 1457: Bekynton no. 1097.

Arundell, Sybil d': oratory at *Sutton Montis* with fit chaplain, Dec 1353 until Easter: Ralph no. 2785.

Attewater, Master J, notary public, and Emmota his wife: any chapel or oratory in his houses in diocese, Mar 1479: Stillington & Fox no. 667.

Badecombe, John and Joan de: licence to build an oratory and have a chantry with their own priest, because of the distance from parish church at *Long Ashton*, saving its rights, 1315: Droxford p. 95.

Barton, John de: in his house [no placed named] by fit priest, Jan 1332, 1 year: Ralph no. 344.

---

[1] John Hacheford and Margaret his wife were allowed by the Apostolic Penitentiary to have masses in the chapel of St James, Stone, in East Pennard, in 1392: *Supplications ... in the Registers of the Apostolic Penitentiary*, i. no. 1392.

Barton, John de: in his chapel at *Woodborough* in *Winscombe*, Oct 1343, 1 year: Ralph no. 1172.

Barton, John de: in oratory of *Woodborough* and *Winterhead* in *Winscombe*, Michaelmas 1353-4: Ralph no. 2793.

Barton, Master William de, rector of Kelston, Dec 1335, licence to celebrate at *Barton*, 2 Years: Ralph no. 956.

Beauchamp, Dame Cecily de, and her son John: to have William de Bath as domestic chaplain provided he visits his parish, gives alms to poor 'etc', Dec 1319: Droxford p. 139.

Beauchamp, Dame Eleanor: chapel or oratory in her house at *Whitelackington*, or in any other place in diocese set apart for divine worship, during pleasure, Feb 1462: Bekynton, no 1414.

Beauchamp of Somerset, Margaret: in chapel at *Merifield* in *Ilton*, Mar 1354, 1 year: Ralph, no 279.

Berghes, Juliana de: oratory at *Berrow*; Feb 1339 until Michaelmas: Ralph no. 1429.

Berkeley, William, knight, lord of Berkeley, and Joan his wife: chapel or oratory in any suitable place in the diocese by 'meet' chaplain, without prejudice to any parish church, July 1476: Stillington & Fox no. 630.

Berthon, John de, wife and free family: licence to build wooden altar with consecrated portable altar on it for chantry in his house, possibly in *Wells*, Nov 1320: Droxford p. 184.

Bluet, John, esquire, and his wife, oratories [no places named], Jan 1404, 1 year: Giffard & Bowett no. 151.

Boef, William, Edith his wife and Edith, his wife's mother: chapel or oratory or 'other honourable place' in manor of *Merriott* during bishop's pleasure, without prejudice to others, May 1457: Bekynton no. 1046.

Bourne, Elizabeth de: chantry for herself and family in oratory or chapel in her house at *Bourne*, without prejudice to the parish church of *Wrington*, Oct 1333, 1 year: Ralph no. 605; oratory at *Bourne* for herself and free family, Nov 1337, 1 year: Ralph no. 1173.

Bracton, Robert de: chantry for self and family in oratory or portable altar at **Bratton** in **Minehead**, but attendance at parish church on four great feasts, June 1317, 2 years: Droxford p. 128.

Bret, John le: oratory at *Thorncombe* in *Bicknoller*; July 1334, 1 year: Ralph no. 688.

Brompton, Andrew de: himself and free family, chapel of the manor of *Walton in Gordano*, Feb 1334 to Pentecost, without prejudice: Ralph no. 655); chapel at *Walcott* (*Walton*), May 1338 to Michaelmas: Ralph no. 1210.

Burgh, Elizabeth de, lady of Clare, 'free chantry' anywhere in diocese, Apr 1325: Droxford p. 244.

Burgh, John de, rector of Huish Champflower: chapel or oratory in his rectory at *Huish* by fit chaplain, 1 year without prejudice to his church, June 1408: Bubwith no 87.

Burton, John de: chantry in the chapel at *Burton*, chaplain to swear allegiance annually to mother church of *Curry Rivel*, Oct 1322: Droxford p. 207.

Burton, Richard de: had papal bull licensing a chapel at *Burton* in *Curry Rivel* and allowing a chaplain, no date given: Droxford p. 207.

Canon, Master Ralph, canon of Wells: all his oratories in diocese, May 1402: Giffard & Bowett no. 73.

Canyng, William, Joan his wife, William their son, and Isabel his wife: 'any place fit' in his house in *St Mary Redcliffe parish*, Bristol, during bishop's pleasure without prejudice to others' rights, May 1454: Bekynton no. 841.

Cheigne, William de: because of the illness of his wife, oratory in their manor house at *Wellow*, revocable at instance of Richard de Plymstock, saving rights of mother church, July 1315: Droxford p. 90.

Cheleworth, Adam de, citizen of Wells: chapel or oratory built within his dwellings at Wells, Oct 1337, 1 year: Ralph no. 1164.

Cherleton, Sir Alan de: chantry in manorial chapel by own priest, far from church of *Rode*, Mar 1324: Droxford p. 230.

Chilthorne Vag, John of: chantry in oratory when unable to reach church at *Chilthorne Domer*, by own priest, Apr 1321: Droxford p. 187.

Chippeley, Thomas, *domicellus*: to have masses in unnamed oratories, Jan 1404, 1 year: Giffard & Bowett no. 153.

Clyvedon, Richard de: chapel at *Potyngthrop* in *Banwell*,[1] Oct 1339, 1 year: Ralph no. 1370.

Cogan, Richard, knight: chapel at *Huntspill*, Nov 1334 until Michaelmas: Ralph no. 726.

Coker, Nicholas, esquire: oratory in *Yeovil* with portable altar, 1 year, Sept 1414: Bubwith no. 504.

Coker, Richard: oratory at *West Bower* in *Bridgwater*, Sept 1339, 1 year: Ralph no. 1363.

Coker, Robert, esquire and Agnes his wife: portable altar, *Lydeard St Laurence*, without prejudice to parish church or rector, 1 year, Nov 1418: Bubwith no. 808.

Coker, William: chapel or oratory at *West Bower* in *Bridgwater*, Dec 1334 during illness by suitable chaplain provided no prejudice to parish church: Ralph no. 729.

Combe, wife of William de: broken with age, hallowed super-altar in her chamber, saving rights of *Stogumber* church, Feb 1325: Droxford p. 240.

Cornu, William, esquire, and Joan his wife: portable altar anywhere in diocese, during pleasure, Oct 1422: Bubwith no. 1129.

Cotes, Robert, and his wife Elizabeth and household servants: chapel or oratory in their house at *Allery* in *Wiveliscombe* and elsewhere in diocese during pleasure by suitable chaplain, probably Oct 1453: Bekynton no. 784.

Courtenay, Joan, widow: oratory or other suitable place by suitable chaplain, in her manor of *Withycombe*, during pleasure, provided no prejudice to *Withycombe* parish church, Aug 1449: Bekynton no. 442.

Craucombe, Simon de: oratory at *Leigh* in *Crowcombe*, Feb 1343, 1 year: Ralph no. 18.

Crosse, William: oratory at *Tetton* in *Kingston St Mary*, 1 year, Apr 1411: Bubwith no. 294.

---

[1] The chapel of St George, which became the district of St Georges: S. Rippon, *Landscape, Community and Colonisation: the North Somerset Levels during the 1st to 2nd millennia AD* (Council for British Archaeology, Research Report 152, 2006), 106-8. I owe this reference to David Bromwich.

Dawbeney, Giles, esquire, lord of Barrington, his wife and domestic servants: chapel or oratory in *Barrington*, in a low voice, March 1415: Bubwith no. 537.

Dedyngton, Thomas, esquire: his oratory in *Wellington* with portable altar, 'without prejudice, etc.', 1 year, Sept 1414: Bubwith no. 502.

Enethorn, John, *domicellus*: his oratories, unnamed, in diocese, 20 Oct 1403, 1 year: Giffard & Bowett no. 130.

Eorul (?), Sir William, esquire (sic) and Lady Margaret Malet, his wife: any suitable place in diocese 'set in order for divine worship', during pleasure without prejudice to anyone, May 1425: Stafford no. 38.

Esse (Eisset), Joan, widow of Matthew de: at her mansion at *Cudworth*, May 1333, by suitable chaplain with no prejudice to parish church: Ralph no. 558.

Fienles, Sir John de, lord of Martock: divine service chapel at *Martock* by fit chaplain, Nov 1334: Ralph no. 715.

Fitzjames, John, esquire, and Alice his wife: chapel or oratory at *Redlynch* in *Bruton* or other suitable place in diocese, during pleasure, Jan 1459: Bekynton no. 1187.

Fitzpayn, Juliana, widow of Elias: manorial chapel at *Alhampton* in *Ditcheat*, Oct 1337, 1 Year: Ralph, no. 1159.

Fitzpayn, Margery la: oratory at *Churchill*, May 1339 until Easter: Ralph no. 1329.

Flory, Edmund, esquire: his unnamed oratories in diocese, Nov 1403, 1 year: Giffard & Bowett no. 135.

Forde, Richard de, canon of Wells: oratory in house at *Wells* and elsewhere in diocese on consecrated super-altar, Nov 1320: Droxford p. 184.

Foxe, William: in his dwelling in *Stoke sub Hamdon* 'so long as his present bodily infirmity lasts', Mar 1459: Bekynton no, 1196.

Fraunceys, Eleanor, widow, and household: chapel or oratory in manor of *Combe Florey* or at other suitable places in diocese, without prejudice to others' rights, January 1454: Bekynton no. 813.

Fry, Thomas, esquire, and Sybil his wife: chapel or oratory in their dwelling in *St John the Baptist parish, Glastonbury* by suitable chaplain during pleasure, without prejudice to parish church, Feb 1473: Stillington & Fox no. 565.

Gambon, Joan, widow of Robert Gambon: chapel or oratory or other suitable place in *Buckland St Mary* by 'any chaplain of her choice', March 1498: King & Hadrian no. 71.

Gerbarston, John de, wife and free family: chapel in his court at *Gerbeston* in *West Buckland* by suitable priest without prejudice to parish church, Mar 1333, 1 year: Ralph no. 538.

Gireldston, John de, layman: disabled from reaching church, chantry on consecrated super-altar, Mar 1321, 1 year: Droxford p. 186

Glastingbury, Sir Henry de: chantry in his manor house, unnamed, revocable, Sept 1316: Droxford p. 112.

Godewyn, William: oratory at *Bishop's Lydeard*, Oct 1404, 1 year: Giffard & Bowett no. 194.

Godwyn, John, gentleman, and Joan his wife: chapel or oratory in their house in *Wells* during pleasure, provided no prejudice to others, Dec 1458: Bekynton no. 1175.

Gosse, William, of *Bridgwater*, and wife: 'any place within the diocese arranged for divine worship', 1 year, Apr 1411: Bubwith no. 293.

Gregory, Walter de, chaplain: in house of Robert Wellyngton *by Taunton*, in low voice by fit chaplains, 1 year, Dec 1416: Bubwith no. 668.

Grindenham, William de, wife, and household: because of age and the distance of the parish church of *Kittisford*, in their chapel at *Greenham*, on a super-altar by priest at own cost, not to be prejudicial to the parish church, Sept 1316: Droxford p. 112.

Guldene, Roger de (or le) and Elizabeth, chapel of the Blessed Katherine in their court at *Milborne Wick* in *Milborne Port*, Mar 1332: Ralph no. 355; to same and free family, Jan 1334 to Michaelmas: Ralph no. 642; June 1338, 2 years: Ralph no. 1226.

Halsewell, Katherine: oratory in *Goathurst* parish, Nov 1476: Stillington & Fox no. 645.

Halsewell, William de: super-altar in oratory in *Halswell Court* in *Goathurst* by his chaplain, Sept 1318: Droxford p. 17.

Hampton, Egelina de, for self and free family: chamber in manor house at *Badgworth*, Dec 1333 to Lent 1334: Ralph no. 630; oratory in manor house, *Badgworth*, Mar 1334, 1 Year: Ralph no. 656.

Harowe, Master J, vicar of North Petherton: chapels or oratories in diocese by suitable chaplains, Mar 1498: King & Hadrian no. 76.

Haule, Thomas, rector of Charlton Musgrove: chapel of St Stephen in his rectory house on portable altar in a low voice, 1 year, Nov 1418: Bubwith no. 812.

Heighe, Amice de la (atte): chapel of *La Heighe* in *Winsham*, Feb 1338, 2 years: Ralph no, 1227; same at oratory at *La Heighe*, Dec 1343, 1 year: Ralph no. 1776.

Hille, Robert, abbot of Athelney: in any chapels or oratories in diocese 'set apart for divine worship, no prejudice to parish churches, during pleasure, June 1462: Bekynton no. 1442.

Hombre, John de: oratory at *Hummer* in *Trent*, Feb 1344, 1 year: Ralph no. 1826.

Hoper, Stephen, merchant: chapel or oratory or other suitable place in his house in *Yeovil* because of bodily weakness, by suitable chaplain, provided *Yeovil* church does not suffer, June 1448: Bekynton no. 348.

Hore, Thomas and his wife Joan: chapel or oratory or other suitable place in their house in *Holy Cross Temple parish*, *Bristol*, because of 'great age and bodily weakness, with fit chaplain, provided no prejudice to parish church, December 1463: Bekynton no. 1538.

Horsted, Alice de, her family and a paralytic, Robert Molyns: licence to erect in her manor house at *Milborne Wick* in *Milborne Port* 'a super-altar, consecrated, upon wooden tabula'; for life if not revoked, her chaplain to respect parish church, Feb 1314: Droxford p. 163.

Hulle, Robert: all his oratories in the diocese, during pleasure, Dec 1401: Giffard & Bowett no. 24.

Hulle, Robert, esquire, and Elizabeth his wife: oratory in their manor house at *Spaxton*, Oct 1408, at the vicar-general's will: Giffard & Bowett no. 350; Bubwith no, 111.

Hundon, Thomas, vicar of Chard, his household domestics: papal indult for portable altar, Oct 1428: Stafford no. 32.

Huscarl, Alexandra: chantry in oratory in manor house at *Eastrip* in *Bruton*, served by own priest with a consecrated portable super altar, saving rights of parish church, Mar 1320: Droxford p. 148.

Husee, James and wife: oratory at *Bathampton*, Mar 1354 until Michaelmas during sickness by vicar of Bathampton: Ralph no. 2815.

Hymmerford, John and Joan his wife: any chapel or oratory in their houses in diocese, Mar 1479: Stillington & Fox no. 667.

15 Hymerford house, East Coker: reproduced from Batten's *South Somerset Villages* by John Batten (Somerset Books, 1994), opp. p. 169

Inge, Sir John, wife and free family: oratory at *Downhead* in *Doulting*, Nov 1343: Ralph no. 1763.

Inge, Sir John: chapel at *Corston*, Mar 1344, 1 year: Ralph no. 1822.

Iressch, Margery le: chapel in *Badgworth*, Apr 1332, 1 year: Ralph no. 389.

Iressch, Margery la: chapel at *Middletone*, May 1332, 1 year: Ralph no. 389.

Ismania[1], lady of Coity: in her manor of *Owle Knowle* in *Carhampton*, 1 year, Aug 1413: Bubwith no. 428.

Jacob, Martin and Joan his wife: in chapels, oratories and other suitable places within their mansion house, which is about a mile from *North Petherton* church and 'they are unable on account of age to attend there to hear divine service as often as they would wish'; by any suitable chaplain, Nov 1443: Bekynton no. 17.

Jerard, John, esquire, and Joan his wife: chapel or oratory in their house at *Sandford Orcas* 'and in all places in the diocese set apart for divine worship', during pleasure provided no prejudice to any parish church, June 1462: Bekynton no. 1436.

Keel, Humphrey de: chapel at *Walterescomb* in *Chard*, Oct 1334, 1 year: Ralph no. 718.

Ken, Elizabeth, wife of John de, altar and super-altar in her chamber at *Kenn*, July 1333, 6 Weeks: Ralph no. 682.

Kenne, John, or household: oratory in dwelling place of *Cannington*, in low voice by fit chaplain, 1 year, without prejudice to parish church, Oct 1417: Bubwit, no. 717.

Knygth, John, wife and free family: oratory at *Castle Cary*, Nov 1343, 1 year: Ralp, no. 1762.

Kynardeley, William, canon of Wells: oratory at *Wells*, April 1354, 1 year: Ralph no. 2828.

Langebrok, Robert and Christian his wife: chapel or decent oratory in the dwelling house of John Warmwelle at *Newton Surmaville* in *Yeovil* parish, Oct 1411: Bubwith no. 312.

Langebrugge, Hugh de and wife, altar in his mansion in *Bristol*, May 1332: Ralph no. 403.

Lannoy, John, esquire, and his wife: oratory, 'decent and arranged for divine worship' in his manor in *Cloford*, in low voice, without prejudice to anyone, 1 year, Feb 1419: Bubwith no. 831.

---

[1] She was Ismania de Hanham, widow of Sir Laurence de Berkerolles.

Legyr, Roger: consecrated super-altar in manorial chapel at *Bishopsworth*; mass by his own chaplain, Apr 1316, 'until the bishop comes into neighbourhood': Droxford p. 11.

Lodhuish, John de: to build an oratory with wooden sub-altar and portable super-altar, consecrated, at *Lodhuish* in *Nettlecombe* and to hear mass, Sept 1318: Droxford p.18.

Lodehiwissch, John de: oratory at *Lodhuish* in *Nettlecombe*, before self and free family by suitable chaplain, July 1334, 1 year: Ralph no. 688.

Luccombe, Geoffrey de: chantry in court at *Luccombe* served at own cost, saving right of mother church, Aug 1316: Droxford p. 110.

Ludes, Robert de, priest, and free family: oratory in dwelling house at *West Bradley* in *East Pennard*, Oct 1345, for life: Ralph no. 1920.

Lutleton, Master William de, precentor of Wells: oratory at *Lutleton* for himself and free family, Jan 1344: Ralph no. 1796.

Luttrell, John, esquire, and Joan his wife: chapel or oratory in his dwelling at *Carhampton*, 1 year, July 1419: Bubwith no. 875.

Malet, Sir Baldwin and wife: oratory at manor at *Enmore*, Aug 1404, 1 year: Giffard & Bowett no. 184.

Malet, Sir Baldwin, knight or Avice his wife: anywhere in diocese 'apt for this and of good repute', by fit chaplain, 1 year, Apr 1412: Bubwith no. 335; renewed Sept 1413: Bubwith no. 431; renewed to **Malet** as **lord of Enmore**, Mar 1415: Bubwith no. 538.

Malherbe, William de: oratory in manor house at *Standerwick* by priest approved by bishop, during pleasure, saving rights of parish church of *Frome*, Nov 1311: Droxford p. 46.

Marchaunt, John or his wife: oratory in his dwelling house in *Taunton*, 1 year, Aug 140: Bubwith no. 95.

Martyn, Edmund and wife: chapel at *Wythicombe*, to celebrate on super-altar by a chaplain, June 1318 for life: Droxford p. 13.

Martyn, Robert, wife and free family: oratory at *Pipelpenne*, Jan 1344, 1 year: Ralph no. 1798.

Martyn, Robert: Walter Pope to celebrate in his oratory [place not named] Dec 1351 until Michaelmas: Ralph no. 2619.

Mede, Philip and his wife Isabel: chapel or oratory in their house in the parish of *St Mary Redcliffe*, Bristol, and in other suitable, but unnamed places in the diocese, provided no prejudice to others' rights, February 1458: Bekynton no. 1115.

Meriet, Sir John: chantry in chapel of manor house at *Hestercombe*, mother church of *Cheddon* too far, July 1316: Droxford p. 109.

Meryet, Simon de: divine service in chapel at *Hestercombe* in *Cheddon FitzPaine*, Mar 1354 until Michaelmas: Ralph no. 2822.

Molton, Sir John de, his wife and free family: chapel at *Wellington* by fit chaplain, Dec 1343 1 year: Ralph no. 1770.

Montacute, William de, earl of Salisbury, and Alice: altar in manor house at *Donyatt*; bishop of Exeter is licensed to consecrate, Oct 1339: Ralph no. 1368.

Montagu, William, gentleman: chapel or oratory with portable altar in dwelling at *Henley* in *Crewkerne parish*, Oct 1473: Stillington & Fox no. 587.

More, John atte: house at *Birdcombe* with wooden altar and super-altar, Sept 1331, 1 year without prejudice to *Wraxall* parish church: Ralph no. 286.

Moreton, Master John, canon of Wells: oratory of his dwelling or elsewhere in diocese, without prejudice to others, Aug 1450: Bekynton no. 524.

Moretone, John and Alice de: chapel of St James, *Morton* in *Compton Martin*, May 1332, 5 Years: Ralph no. 395.

Moris, Sir J, and household: chantry in manor house at *Faulkland* in *Hemington*, void if prejudicial to parish church, Nov 1311: Droxford p. 46.

Moulton, John: chapel or oratory in *Norton St Philip*, March 1498: King & Hadrian no. 77.

Mulburne, Sir William de, his wife and free family: manorial chapel at *Wydecomb* in *Corston* from Michaelmas 1333, without prejudice to parish church: Ralph no. 489.

Newton, John, knight, and Isabel his wife: chapel or oratory in any suitable place in diocese by a 'meet' chaplain without prejudice to any parish church, July 1476: Stillington & Fox no. 631.

North, Master William, vicar of North Curry: in his vicarage house at *North Curry* and 'in any other places ordained for divine worship' in the diocese by self or another, provided no prejudice to any parish church, Jan 1448: Bekynton no. 322.

Osbourn, Walter, vicar of Frome: his house in *Frome* and anywhere else in the diocese, without prejudice to others' rights, Nov 1449: Bekynton no. 466.

Othery, Thomasina, widow of Richard, and her domestics: oratory at *Holnicote* in *Selworthy*, 1 year, by any fit chaplains, May 1413: Bubwith no. 415.

Palton, Lady Elizabeth: portable altar in chapel or oratory in her manor of *Croscombe* during pleasure, May 1422: Bubwith no. 1096.

Paulet, Elizabeth, and her household: oratories [unnamed] within the diocese by fitting chaplains, Nov. 1401: Giffard & Bowett no. 9.

Pavely, Sir Walter: oratory at *Tellisford*, July 1344 until Christmas: Ralph nos. 1418, 1851.

Pedewel, Agnes: chapel or oratory or suitable place in her house in *Wells* because of age and bodily weakness by chaplain, provided no prejudice to her parish church, June 1452: Bekynton no. 665.

Peter, vicar of Queen Camel, oratory in his vicarage house at *Queen Camel*, Nov 1343, 1 year, by self or another: Ralph no. 1762.

Plokenet, Sybil: oratory in house of John Baret in *Montacute* for herself and free family, Mar 1344, 1 year: Ralph no. 1822.

Poer, Henry: to have divine service in 'any suitable place in the court of William de Lottesham' in *Lottisham* in *Ditcheat*, May 1333, 1 year: Ralph no. 559.

Poulet, John, his wife and free family: oratory in *Pawlett*, Jan 1344, 1 year: Ralph no. 1797.

Ralegh, Joan de, widow: chantry in chapel in manor house of *Rowdon* in *Stogumber*, revocable at will or if prejudicial to parish church, July 1316: Droxford p. 109.

Ralee, Joan de, self and free family: oratory at *Rowdon* in *Stogumber*, July 1334, 2 years: Ralph no. 688.

Rede, Thomas: oratory in his dwelling at *Bristol*, 1 year, Sept 1409: Bubwith no. 167.
Reigni, John de: chapel at *Rhode*, by own chaplain because of distance from parish church at *North Petherton* and floods, voided if prejudicial, May 1316: Droxford p. 108.
Rodney, Sir Walter and his wife Isabella: all oratories in diocese, Mar 1402: Giffard & Bowett no. 52.
Roland, John, canon of Wells: chapel or oratory in his house in *Wells*, bishop's pleasure, Nov 1410: Bubwith nos. 53, 265.
Ryuere, John de la: suitable chapel at *Wyke* in *Compton Dando*, Feb 1334 during pleasure: Ralph no. 651.
Sampford, Hugh, and Maud his wife: chapel or oratory, at *Bakhey*, in low voice by fit chaplain, without prejudice to parish church, Aug 1416: Bubwith no. 639.
Samuel, Geoffrey: chapel at *Luckington* in *Kilmersdon* approved by the prioress of Minchin Buckland, 1301, to be served by vicar of Kilmersdon: Droxford p. 294.
Samuel, William: chantry at *Luckington* in *Kilmersdon*, Nov 1328: Droxford p. 294.
Say, John, wife and free family: oratory at *Martock*, May 1333, 1 year, no prejudice to parish church: Ralph no. 558.
Saymour, Roger, esquire, and his wife Margaret: oratory in manor house at *Hatch Beauchamp*, Oct 1408, at vicar-general's pleasure: Giffard & Bowett no. 351, Bubwith no 112.
Seyncler, Robert: chapel at *Stapleton* in *Martock*, Nov 1334: Ralph no. 724.
Seyntcler, Robert: oratory in his mansion at *Butleigh*, Jan 1344, for 1 year by fit chaplain: Ralph no. 1793.
Seynt John, Edward, esquire, and household: oratory or chapel in house at *Selworthy*, without prejudice to others' rights, Oct 1456: Bekynton no. 1006.
Sherp, John and household: oratory or other suitable place in his manor of *Charlton* in *Portbury* parish, Sept 1454: Bekynton no. 880.
Slo, John atte: oratory at *Slough* in *North Curry*, Dec 1337, 1 year: Ralph no. 1190.
Stafford, Humphrey, esquire, and Isabel his wife: chapel, oratory or 'other suitable chamber' in *Taunton Castle*, and in 'other

places in the diocese set apart for divine worship', during pleasure, Jan 1461: Bekynton no. 1355.

St Loe (Seyntlou), John: chapel at *Newton*, May 1332, 1 year: Ralph no. 385.

St Loe (Seynlowe), John, esquire, and his wife: oratory in his dwelling house at *Bechewstoke*, 1 year, Oct 1412: Bubwith no. 374; renewed for 1 year, to be said 'in a subdued voice' Feb 1414: Bubwith no. 479.

Stokes, Master John, canon of Wells: mass in his house in *Wells* or anywhere else in diocese, without prejudice, Sept 1449: Bekynton no. 1445.

Stradelyng, Elizabeth, relict of Edward and household: chapel or oratory, 'in a low voice' at *Halsway* without prejudice to *Crowcombe* church, Oct 1415: Bubwith no. 578.

Sutton, Richard and his wife Alice: all oratories or chapels in diocese by fit chaplains, Apr 1402: Giffard & Bowett no. 69.

Sutton, William de: chapel at *Hinton Blewett*, by Adam, the rector of *Hinton*, Oct 1349 until Christmas: Ralph no. 2406.

Sydenham, Henry and Richard, esquires: oratories, by fit chaplains, pleasure, Feb 1402: (Giffard & Bowett no. 44.

Todenham, Robert de, clerk: chapel of his manor or house at *Lymington* by fit priests, Nov 1332: Ralph no. 47.

Towker, John, vicar in Wells cathedral: oratory in his house in *Vicars' Close*, daily in low voice, Dec 1497: King & Hadrian no. 57.

Trew, Thomas, esquire, his wife and household: chapels or oratories, in low voice by fit chaplains in manors of *Plainsfield* and *Vexford*, without prejudice to parish churches, 1 year, Jan 1417: Bubwith no. 686; repeated Sept 1417: Bubwith no. 715.

Trowe, John and his wife Agnes, servants and household: chapel or oratory or suitable place in manor of *Plainsfield*, provided no prejudice to parish church of *Over Stowey*, during bishop's pleasure, Sept 1447: Bekynton no. 290.

Tylly, Leonard, esquire, and Joan his wife: chapel at *Withiel*, without prejudice to parish church of *Cannington*, during pleasure, Feb 1460: Bekynton no. 1285.

Appendix III: Oratories and Chapels

Wadham, J, esquire, and Isabel his wife, of *Whitelackington*: any chapel or oratory in diocese, Oct 1477: Stillington & Fox no. 648.

Wadham, Katharine, widow: chapel or oratory in her manor of *Preston* in *Yeovil*, or in other suitable places in diocese by a chaplain, provided no prejudice to other parish churches, Nov 1452: Bekynton no. 698.

Walton, Petronilla de: chapel in manor house at *Hemington*, Mar 1334 until Michaelmas: Ralph no. 656.

Wike, John: oratory at *Wyke* in *Yatton*, Apr 1338, 1 year: Ralph no. 1200.

Wild, Richard le: chantry at *Dunwear* in *North Petherton*, Sept 1316: Droxford p. 112 (corrected).

Wymyate, Peter atte: oratory at *Perry* in *East Quantoxhead*, fit chaplain, Feb 1343, 1 year: Ralph no. 1811.

Yenston, John: oratory at *Yenston* in *Henstridge*, Jan 1339 to Michaelmas: Ralph no. 1314.

INDEX OF PERSONS AND PLACES

Places are in Somerset unless otherwise stated
Abp – archbishop; bp – bishop; Mr – Master; r – rector;
v – vicar

Abbot's Leigh, 74
Abraham, Agnes, 50
Acre, St Thomas's hospital, 111
Acton, Thomas de, 54
Adam, r of Hinton Blewett
Adscombe, see Stowey, Over
Agincourt (France), battle, 99–100
Alampton, John, 60
Alampton, John, vicar in Wells cathedral, 119
Alan, messenger, 3
Aleton, Thomas de l', r of Spaxton, 110
Alexander the barber, 77
Alhampton, see Ditcheat
Aller, 27; Oath, 45; r of, see Clyvedon
Allercote, William, 19
Allery, see Wiveliscombe
Alresford, Robert de, canon of Taunton, 20
Amesbury (Wilts), abbey, 93
Ammercy, Gilbert, 54
Ap Aaron, Elizabeth and her husband Sir Thomas, 57
Apperleigh, John, 119
Aquitaine (France), 95, 99, 118
Arnall, Clemence, 56
Arthur, Cecily, widow of William, 119
Arundell, Sybil d', 119

Ashmorebrook, Walkelin de, r of Chedzoy, 22, 64
Ashton, Long, 119
Ashwick, 19
Assh, John, 55
Athelney: abbey, 6, 37–8, 115; abbey church, 116; abbot of, see Hille
Attemede, John, r of Seavington St Michael, 30
Attemore, of Chedzoy, 34; Jn, 18
Attenayssh, John, 18
Atteslape, Nicholas, of Chedzoy, 34
Attewater, Mr John and Emmota his wife, 119
Audley, Lord, 53
Avignon (France), 46, 110–11
Axbridge, 59, 73, 82; r of, 104; rural dean, 59

Backwell, 35; r of, see Pykeslegh
Bacon, John, 47
Badecombe, John and Joan de, 119
Badgworth: chapel, 54, 126; manor house, oratory, 125
Bagborough, 46
Bagshot (Surr), inn, 4
Baker: John, 21; Jn the, mayor of Bath, 73
Bakheye, chapel in, 131
Ballard: Joan, 58; John, 58

Bannockburn (Scotland), battle, 93
Banwell, 48, 57–8, 60, 63–4, 80, 82, 87; chapel, 80, 102; church, 58, 64; manor chapel, 58, 62; Potyngthrop, chapel, 122 and n; v of, see Gernesey; and see Churchill
Baret, John, 130
Barkle, see Berkeley
Barlinch, priory, 37–8, 115
Barlow, William, bp of Bath & Wells, register, 9n
Barnet, John, bp of Bath & Wells, 9
Barre: John de la, 58; Laurence de la, r of Compton Martin, 58, 123
Barrow, North, r of, see Faryngdon
Barrow, priory, 37–8
Barton: John de, 119–20; Mr William, r of Kelston, 120
Barton, 120
Basel, Council, 112
Baskerwyle, Humphrey, 19
Basset, Edm, 19; (John and William), 18
Batcombe, 27, 50n
Batecomb, Nicholas de, 27
Bath: Nicholas de, 3; William de, 120; William of, r of Swainswick, vicar choral of Wells cathedral, 31
Bath, cathedral priory, 6, 8, 36n, 37, 58, 73, 115–16; monks, 76; prior of, 82, and see Byrde, Iford
Bath: archdeacon of, 89, and see Pykman; archdeaconry, 7, 109
Bath, city: 53, 56, 70, 73, 82; bridge, 116; gaol, 73; hospital, 116; market, 73; mayor, see Baker, Hogekyns; school, 107; St John's hospital, 6; St Mary Stalls, 74; St Michael's, 73; streets, 73–4; townsmen, 73; Trinity pilgrimage, 49
Bathampton, 42; oratory at, 126
Bathford, 82

Bathwick, 68
Battlefield (Salop), 116; chapel, 98
Bavaria, Louis (Lewis) of, emperor, 111
Bawdewyn, Isabel, 56
Bayeux (France), 118
Beauchamp (of Somerset): Cecily and her son, James, 120; Eleanor, 120; Sir John de, 79; Margaret, 120; Richard, earl of Warwick, 99
Bechewstoke, see Chewstoke
Beckington, 28, 50, 61; r of, 31, and see Fabell
Bedell, William, 19
Bedford, John, duke of, 100
Bedfordshire, see Felmersham
Bedminster, 21, 69, 74, 119; Bishopsworth, manor chapel, 128
Beercrocombe, 70; church, 86
Beere, Richard, abbot of Glastonbury, 39
Bekynton, Thomas, bp of Bath & Wells, 4–5, 28–31, 38–9, 42–4, 48–9, 60, 62, 68, 70, 74, 76, 78, 80, 87, 90, 101, 103; household, 21; register, 9, 20, 77, 79, 82–3, 86
Bele: Anys, 58; Henry, 58; Thomas, priest, 58; Thomas, father of Thomas, 58
Benedict XII, pope, 109
Benedict XIII, anti-pope, 111
Benet, John, 34
Berghes, Juliana de, 120
Berkeley (Barkle, Berkley): Sir Maurice, 58; Thomas de, 58; Sir William, and Joan his wife, 120
Berkeley (Glos), 120
Berkerolles, Sir Laurence de, 127n
Berkley (Som), 70
Berkshire, 39; and see Bisham, Compton, Windsor
Bernard, Jn, r of Claverton, 29
Berrow: oratory in, 120; r of, 27

Berthon, John de, 120
Bery, William, 21
Beverley, St John of, 99
Bewel (William), 19
Bicknoller, Thorncombe in, 121
Birdcombe, see Wraxall
Bisham (Berks), priory, 23
Bishop's Hull, 21, 69
Bishop's Lydeard, oratory, 124
Bishop's Sutton, 56
Bishopsworth, see Bedminster
Bisse (Bysse), Philip, 19
Bisshop, Jn, 55
Bithewell (Ric), 19
Bitton (Bytton): Sir John, 58; John, his son, 58; William of, I, bp of Bath & Wells, 7, 22, 84, 88; William of, II, bp of Bath & Wells, 7
Bitton (Glos), church, 58
Blachyngdon, Willelma de, prioress of Cannington, 20
Blackford, 42
Blackford (in Wedmore), 80, 82, 83; chapel, 105
Blagdon, 59
Bleadney, see Wookey
Bleadon, church, 85; r of, 46
Bluet, John, 120
Bode, William de, 73
Boef, William, Edith his wife, and Edith, his wife's mother, 120
Boggere, Richard, 54
Bois, Henry de, r of Timsbury, 29
Boniface IX, pope, 109
Bonville, Sir William, 4, 100
Bordeaux (France), 64, 102
Bosworth (Leics), battle, 104
Bothe, John, and his widow Alice, 55
Boulogne (France), 106
Bourne, see Wrington
Bourne; Elizabeth de, 120; Gilbert, bp of Bath & Wells, 107; register, 51, 107, 113; seal, 16; Tho, 45

Bouwney, John, elder, 50
Bower, West, see Bridgwater
Bowerman, William, registrar, 13, 15
Bowet, Henry, bp of Bath & Wells, 13, 98; register, 9, 14, 69, 98
Bracton, Robert de, 120
Bradley, West, see Pennard, East
Bratton, see Minehead
Braunston: Ellen, wife of William, 99, 118; Hugh, 99; Robert, 118; William de, 99, 118
Braye: Robert, 55; William, 55
Breane, r of, 99
Brent, Robert, 99, 118
Brent, East, 56
Bret, John le, 121
Bridgwater, 34, 43, 53, 74, 103, 124; causeway, 116; church, chantry, 74; friary, 87; rural dean, 85; St John's hospital, 38, 115; v of, 46, 56; West Bower, oratory, 43, 56, 122
Brikebet, Henry, monk of Glastonbury, 39, 54
Brislington, 69
Bristol, 45, 47–50, 54, 61, 63, 74, 127, 131; Bowbrigge, 116; bridge, 75; friars, 61, 74; Holy Cross Temple, 34, 48, 50 and n, 74, 125; Lawford's Gate, 49n; mayors, 75, and see Vaughan; St Augustine's abbey, 116; St John's hospital, 38, 74–5; St Katherine's hospital, 48, 116; streets, 58, 75; St Thomas's church, 74–5; and see Redcliffe
Brittany, duke of, 94
Brompton, Andrew de, 121
Browning (Brownybg), Johan, wife of John Mone, 53, 56
Brunstill, Isabel, 58
Brushford, 19; church, 19
Bruton, 34, 46, 59, 75; church of SS Peter and Paul, 64; Eastrip,

Index 137

oratory in, 126; prior of, 27, and see Shoyll; priory, later abbey, 37–9, 85, 115; Redlynch, chapel in, 123
Bruys (la Brus), Beatrice de, and her daughter Joan, 53
Brympsfield (Glos), v of, see Hillesle
Bubwith, Nicholas, bp, 5, 9, 13, 15–16, 29, 38, 47, 61, 64, 72, 74, 80, 91, 98–100, 111–12; register, 9, 111–12
Buckingham (Bucks), 34
Buckinghamshire, see Buckingham, Eton
Buckland Dinham, 50n
Buckland Sororum (Minchin Buckland), 36; prioress, 131
Buckland St Mary, 100; chapel, 124
Buckland, West, 18, 82; Gerbeston, chapel in, 124
Buckton, Thomas, 8
Buclande, Ralph, 19
Burges (Burgeis): Geoffrey, 18; John, 50
Burgh: Elizabeth de, lady of Clare, 121; Hugh de la, 78; Jn de, r of Huish Champflower, 121; Maud de, countess Gloucester, 31
Burnell, Robert, bp of Bath & Wells, 7, 27, 81
Burnett, 56
Burnham, 68; church, 85
Burrington, see Wrington
Burtle, prior of, 9, 87
Burton: John de, 121; Richard de, 121
Burton, see Curry Rivel
Bustell, John, Joan, and John, 58
Butiler (Buteler): Joan, 56; John, 18
Butleigh, mansion, oratory, 131
Byrde, William, prior of Bath, 39
Bytton, see Bitton

Cadbury, John, 62–3
Cadbury, North, 19; r of, 30, 42
Cadbury, South, 50n; chapel, 45, 117
Caen (France), 96
Calais (France), 96–7, 105
Calne, William de, friar, 64
Cambridgeshire, see Molesworth
Camel, Queen: v of, see Peter; vicarage house, oratory, 130
Camme, Nicholas de, 3
Cammel: William, keeper of the palace, 81; William, scribe, 111
Cannington, 62, 86, 127; Blackmoor Fm, 43–4; Gurney Street, 43; priory, 37–8, 62, 115; prioress, see Blachyngdon; v of, 62; Withiel, chapel at, 132
Canon, Mr Ralph, canon of Wells, 121
Canterbury, abp of, 5, 49–50, 77, 94, 97, 105–6, 113, and see Chichele, Courtenay, Cranmer, Pole, Reynolds, Stafford; Prerogative Court of, 57; shrine of St Thomas at, 46, 48
Cantilupe, St Thomas de, 111
Canyng, William, Joan his wife, William their son and Isabel his wife, 121
Capland, church, 70; r of, 70–1
Carent, family, 42
Carhampton: oratory in house, 128; Owle Knowle, manor, 127; v of, 55
Carpenter, John le, 18
Cary, Thomas, escheator, 18
Castello, Hadrian de, bp of Bath & Wells, register, 13
Castillon (France), battle, 102
Castle Cary, 19–20; Cockhill, 18; oratory in, 127; v of, 68
Champflower: Edith, 46; John, 46
Chapman (Chapeman): Adam le, 3; James or John, 59

Chard: Holy Cross chapel, 34; v of, 71 and see Hundon; Watercombe (Walterescomb), chapel in, 127
Charlinch, Gothelney Hall, 43
Charlton, see Portbury, Rode
Charlton Musgrove, 19; chapel of St Stephen in rectory house, 125; r of, 31, and see Haule
Cheddar, 82
Cheddon Fitzpaine, Hestercombe, chapel in manor house, 129
Chedzoy, 21,23–4, 34; r of, 9n, 22; r of, 99, and see Ashmorebrook, Urswick
Cheigne, William de, 121
Cheleworth: Adam de, 121; Maud, 60
Cherde, Robert, 45
Cherleton (Cherlton): Sir Alan de, 121; Thomas de, archdeacon of Wells, 58
Chestre (John), 19
Chew Magna, 56, 82
Chewstoke (Bechewstoke), oratory in, 132
Chewton Keynsham, see Keynsham
Chewton Mendip, 95–6; Emborough, chapel, 85; r of, 85
Chichele, Henry, abp of Canterbury, 99
Chichester, bp of, see Pecock
Chiew, William, 77
Chigwell (or Chilkwell), Robert, registrar, 13
Chillington, 72
Chilterne, Walter de, 26
Chilthorne Domer, Chilthorne Vagg in, 121
Chilthorne Vagg, John of, 121
Chilton Cantelo, r of, 31
Chippeley, Thomas, 121
Chiswick (Mdx), 103
Churchill (in Banwell), 34, 72; oratory, 123
Clare, lady of, see Burgh

Clarence, Thomas, duke of, 99
Claverton, 64, 82; r of, see Bernard
Cleeve, abbey, 36
Cleeve, Old, 42; St Mary's chapel, 61, 117
Clement V, pope, 108, 110
Clement VI, pope, 111
Clement VII, pope, 110
Clerke (Clerk), John, bp of Bath & Wells, 38; register, 9n, 39; seal, 16; Nicholas, 55
Clevedon, 59; church, chapel of St Thomas, martyr, 59; manor, 18; manorial chapel of St Peter, 59; v of, see Thomas
Cloford, manor house, 127; v of, 71
Clopton, Richard, 74
Closworth, 23
Clowesham, William, 19
Clyvedon: Edmund, 59; Emeline, wife of Sir John, 59; Sir John de, 18, 27, 59, 79–80; Matthew de, r of Aller, 27, 59; Sir Matthew, 27, 79; Richard de, 122
Cockhill, see Castle Cary
Cockys, Richard 60; family, 60
Cogan: John de, r of Huntspill, 59; Sir Richard, 64, 122; Petronilla, 59; Sir Thomas, 59, 64
Coity (Mon), lady of, see Hanham
Coke, Rose, 56
Coker: Agnes, wife of Robert, 122; Nicholas, 122; Richard, 43, 122; Robert, 55, 122; William, 43, 54, 122
Coker, East: Hymerford House, 126; v of, 68
Cokkeshale, John de, 58
Cole: Agnes, 55; (or Baker) Thomas, and his wife Agnes, 49
Coleford, see Kilmersdon
Colingham, Richard de, 39
Collard, William, 20
Colyer, Thomas, 56

Colyns, Richard, 75
Combe alias Smyth, Thomas, 55
Combe Florey, chapel, 123
Combe Hay, 18; r of, 4
Combe St Nicholas, 71; church, 84; v of, 68
Combe, William de, 122
Comber, Walter, 48–9
Compostella, 46
Compton (Berks), 79
Compton Bishop, 82; v of, see Ludelowe
Compton Dando, Wyke, chapel in, 131
Compton Martin, Moretone, chapel of St James, 129; r of, see Delabeare
Condray, Peter de, 27
Congresbury, 45, 79, 82, 85, 89
Constance, Council, 111–12
Constantinople, 118
Copleston, Thomas, 19
Cornish, Thomas, bp of Tenos, chancellor of Wells, 63
Cornu, William, and his wife Joan, 122
Corston, 56; chapel in, 126; Wydecomb, manorial chapel, 129
Corton Denham, r of, see Montford
Cotes, Robert, and his wife Elizabeth, 122
Cothelstone, 54
Countisbury (Devon), 56
Courtenay: Christian, 54; Joan, widow, 122; William, abp of Canterbury, 47; family, 31
Coye, Stephen, 21, 45
Cranmer, Thomas, abp Canterbury, 106
Cranmore, West, 42
Craucombe, Simon de, 122
Crecy (France), battle, 96
Crede, John, 45, 60
Creech St Michael, 107; v of, 68

Crewkerne, 25, 45n, 47, 69, 100; chantry, 34 and n; chapel, 45; church, 45; Eastham, 69; Henley, chapel, 129; hermitage, 116; St Reyne, chapel, 116
Crispin, St, 99
Crispinian, St, 99
Croscombe, 42; church, 87; manor house, chapel, 130
Croseman, Thomas, and his father Walter, 59
Crosse: Joan, 19; William, 122
Crowcombe: Halsway, chapel in, 132; Leigh, oratory in, 122
Cudworth, mansion, 123
Culmstock (Colmpstoke), Ralph de, canon of Taunton, 20
Curre, John, 19
Curry Mallet, 103; chapel of St John, 55
Curry Moor, 81
Curry, North: Slough, oratory at, 131; v of, see North; vicarage house, 130
Curry Rivel, 23; Burton, chapel, 121
Cutcombe, 19

Daubeney (Dawbeney): Giles, lord of Barrington, 123; Tamsyn, 46
Dauid, Richard, 34
Decon, Christine, and her father Thomas, 55
Dedyngton, Thomas 123
Deighar, Walter le, 75
Delabeare, see Barre
Delamore, Sir Stephen, 79
Denys, Margaret, 62
Derby: John, 60; John, v of Frome, 60
Despenser, Sir Hugh le, 93–4
Devon, earl of, 103
Devon, 93, and see Countisbury, Exeter, Kingsteignton, Otterton, Polsloe, Witheridge

Devynshyre, John, 56
Ditcheat, 53, 56; Alhampton, manorial chapel, 123; Lottisham, court at, 130
Dodyng, Thomas, 21
Dogmersfield (Hants), 80, 82, 95, 105
Donyatt, 21–2; chapel, 22–3; manor house, chapel, 129; r of, 23–4, and see Wytham
Dorchester (Dorset), 69
Dorset, marquess of, 103
Dorset, see Dorchester, Sandford Orcas, Seaborough, Sherborne, Thorncombe, Trent
Doulting, 72; church, 39
Downhead, oratory at, 126
Draycott, 18, 73, 118
Drayton, Thomas, r of Lydeard St Lawrence, 33
Dreycote, Thomas de, 73
Droxford, John, bp of Bath & Wells, 3–5, 7, 10, 27–30, 43, 45–6, 58, 63–6, 76, 78–80, 84–5, 88, 92–5, 108–9, 111; household, 3; register, 8, 16, 22–3, 32, 69, 76, 81, 85
Dublin (Ireland), abp of, see Yng
Dulcote (in Wells), 18, 89
Dultecote, Thomas of, 27
Dulverton, 69
Dundry, 45, 116
Dunster, priory, 115
Dunwear, see Petherton, North
Dynham, Oliver de, 5
Dyssham, Nicholas, v of St Mary's, Taunton, 63

Earnshill, 23
Eastham, see Crewkerne
Easton (in Wells), 18, 89
Eastrip, see Bruton
Edmund, earl of Kent, 95
Edward I, king, 92
Edward II, king, 92–4, 108

Edward III, king, 94–7
Edward IV, king, 102–3
Edward VI, king, 106–7
Egforton, see Fairoak
Ekyn, John, 60
Elizabeth of York, queen, 113
Elizabeth, countess of Holland and Essex, 92
Ellyott, Mr William, 104
Emayn, William, 47–8
Emborough, see Chewton Mendip
Enethorn, John, 123
Engayne, Richard, 39
Englishcombe, v of, 39
Enmore: 102; church, 61; lord of, see Malet, Baldwin; oratory in manor, 128; r of, 62
Eorul, Sir William, and lady Margaret Malet, his wife, 123
Erghum, Ralph de, bp of Bath & Wells, 3, 9; register, 47
Erle, Richard, 21
Esse (Eisset), Joan, widow of Matthew de, 123
Essex, see Walden
Estimere (Estimer, Estmere): John, 60–1; Thomas, 55; (alias Bonde) William, 55
Eston, Walter, 19
Eton (Bucks), College, 105
Eugenius IV, pope, 109, 113
Evans, John, 58
Evercreech, 68; v of, 67, 71
Evesham, John de, 59
Ewley, Thomas, 30
Exeter (Devon), 55; bp of, 104, and see Grandisson; Quinel; diocese, 5, 32; St Nicholas priory, 116
Exford, 61, 106; r of, 61
Exton, 19; r of, 23, and see Walter

Fabell, Roger, r of Beckington, 31n
Fairoak (Egforton), 70, 109; r of, 70–1

Farleigh Hungerford, 70, 103; castle, 86–7; church, 86–7
Farmborough, 103; r of, see Stafford
Faryngdon, Mr John de, 8
Faukeys, John, 75
Faulkland, see Hemington
Felmersham (Beds), 93
Ffrie, Richard le, priest of Whitelackington, 33
Fienles, Sir John de, lord of Martock, 123
Filton (Glos), 69, 72
Fitz alias Figis, Joan, 55
FitzAdam, Walter, 61
FitzGeldwin, Savaric, bp of Bath, 7
Fitzjames: Alice, wife of John, 123; John, 80, 123
Fitzpaine (Fitzpayn): Elias, 123; John, 79; Juliana, 123; Margery la, 123
Flanders, count of, 97
Florence, 110
Flory, Edmund, 123
Fontell, John, 60
Forde: Henry de, 82; Richard de, canon of Wells, 123
Forde (Dors), abbey, 45
Foregge, John, 50
Forster, Patrick, 19
Fortescu (Fortesku), Sir John, 62–3
Fotheringhay (Northants), 93
Fox (Foxe): Richard bp of Bath & Wells, 13, 39, 105; register, 13; Wm, 123
France, 23–4, 94–6, 99, 100–01, 105–6, 118; and see Agincourt, Aquitaine, Avignon, Bayeux, Bordeaux, Boulogne, Caen, Calais, Castillon, Crecy, Gascony, Harfleur, La Hogue, Mont St Michel, Normandy, Paris, Poitiers, Poitou, Rouen, St Malo
Frankelyn, William, 18
Frauncecys, Eleanor, widow, 123

Freene, Stephen, 50
Frenssh, David, 118
Freshford, 70
Frome: Nicholas, abbot of Glastonbury, 39; Thomas, canon of Wells, 60
Frome, 34, 69–70; Keyford, 103; parish church, 128; rural dean, 61; v of, see Derby, Osbourn; vicarage house, 130; and see Standerwick
Fromond, Geoffrey, abbot of Glastonbury, 109
Fry, Thomas, and his wife Sybil, 124
Fuller: Joan, 99, 118; Thomas, 99, 118
Fykeys (Nicholas), 19

Gambon, Joan, widow of Robert, 124
Gascony, 22, 95
Gasqui, Isuardus, 109
Gaunt, John of, 98
Gauter (Gawter): John, elder and younger, 21; John, 61
Gayton, John, 21
Gerald, John, 61
Gerbarston, John de, 124
Germayn, John, 21
Gernesey (Garnesey), John, v of Banwell, vicar choral of Wells cathedral, 31, 60
Gibbys, Henry, 56
Giffard, Walter, bp of Bath & Wells, 7
Gilbert: Robert, bp of London, 63; r of Goathill, 64
Girelston, John de, 124
Glastingbury, Sir Henry de, 124
Glastonbury, 45, 53; abbey, 36 and n, 37–9, 103, 106, 110, 115; abbots of, 7, 38, 47, 68, 81, 85, 108, and see Beere, Frome, Fromond; monks of, see Brikebet,

Wasyn; St John's parish, chapel, 124; St Katherine's chapel, 117
Gloucester, Humphrey, duke of, 100; countess of, see Burgh
Gloucester, 49, 76
Gloucestershire, 39, and see Berkeley, Bitton, Brympsfield, Filton, Gloucester, Hanham, Newyke, Pucklechurch, St Anne in the Woods, Westbury on Trym, Westerleigh
Glyndwr, Owen, 98
Goatacre, Margaret, 53
Goatacre (Gatesterte), (Wilts), 53
Goathill, 24; r of, see Gilbert
Goathurst, Halswell, oratory in, 124–5
Godalming, John, canon of Taunton, 20
Godele, Dean, 89
Godewyn (Godwyne, Godwyn): James, 58; John, master of Wells, and his wife Joan, 77, 124; John (fl 1525/6), 58; William, 124
Goldcliff (Mon), priory, 95
Golde: John (fl 1341), 25; John (fl 1415), 25; John (d 1555), 25; Robert (fl 1404), 25; Robert (fl 1436), 25; Thomas (fl 1465), 25; Thomas (fl 1480), 25; Thomas (fl 1523), 25; family, 21
Goose Bradon, r of, 71
Gore, John, the elder, 55
Gorges, Theobald, 54
Gosse, William, 124
Grandcombe (Crowcombe), William de, Templar, 39
Granden, Thomas de, r of Seavington St Michael, 31
Grandisson, John de, bp of Exeter, 23, 129
Greenham, see Kittisford
Greenwich, West (Kent), 80
Gregory XII, pope, 111
Gregory, Walter de, 124

Grindenham, William de, 124
Grist, John, 56
Gryg, Richard, 50
Guldene, Roger de (le), and Elizabeth, 124

Habraham, Roger, 50
Hacheford, John and his wife Marg, 119n
Hadrian de Castello, bp of Bath & Wells. 113; register, 105
Hainault, Philippa of, queen, 13n
Hakeluyt, Sir Leonard, 46; Margaret, 45–6
Halidon Hill, battle, 94
Hall, William, 50
Halse, r of, see Putte
Halsewell: Katherine, 124; William de, 125
Halsway, see Crowcombe
Hamelyn, Adam, 74
Hampshire, 2; and see Dogmersfield, Hayling, Southampton, Weyhill, Winchester
Hampton, Egelina de, 125
Hanham, Ismania de, lady of Coity, widow of Sir Laurence de Berkerolles, 127 and n
Hanham (Glos), 58
Hanon, Roger de, 82
Happesford, John, 21
Hardington, r of, 71
Harewell, John, bp of Bath & Wells, 6, 9, 68; register, 47
Harfleur (France), 99, 118
Harowe, Mr J, v of North Petherton, 125
Haselbury Plucknett, 44
Haselbury, St Wulfric of, 44
Haselshaw, Walter, bp of Bath & Wells, 7
Hastings, Sir Edward, 107
Hatch Beauchamp, 117; manor house, oratory, 131

Haule, Thomas, r of Charlton Musgrove, 125
Hawkridge, 66
Hawkwell, r of, 69
Hayling (Hants), priory, 95–6
Hebbes, John, 61; Thomas, 61
Heighe, Amice de la, 125
Heighe, La, see Winsham
Heir (John le), 18
Hemington: chapel, 133; Faulkland, manor house, chantry, 129
Hendy, Alice, 55
Henley, see Crewkerne
Henry IV, king, 98
Henry V, king, 99–100
Henry VI, king, 41, 100, 103, 109
Henry VII, king, 104, 113
Henry VIII, king, 42, 105–6
Henstridge, 42; church, 18, 86; Toomer (Thomere), 18; Turneyate, 18; Yenston, oratory, 133
Henton, Jn, 58
Herbert, William, earl of Huntingdon, 104
Hereford, bp of, 31; diocese, 100
Herefordshire, 102
Hestercombe, see Cheddon Fitzpaine
Heysell, Richard, 58
Heytesbury (Wilts), 110
Hill (Hille): Alice, and her husband John, 61; Richard, 58; Robert, abbot of Athelney, 125
Hillesle, William, v of Brympsfield, 58
Hinton Blewett: chapel at, 132; r of, see Adam
Hinton Charterhouse, 36; priory, 36–7, 111
Hinton St George, r of, 71
Hocton, 82
Hody: Sir Alexander 44n, 56; John, 63; Margaret (nee Coker), 44 and n, 56

Hogekyns, William, mayor of Bath, 74
Holberne, Joan, 56
Holcombe, 50, 68; r of, 71
Holes, Andrew, archdeacon of Wells, 4
Holnicote, see Selworthy
Holton, r of, 30
Holy Land, 22, 46
Hombre, John de, 125
Hoper, Stephen, 125
Hore, Thomas and his wife Joan, 125
Hornblotton, 19, 35
Horsted, Alice de, 43, 125
Hoton alias Pynner, Robert, 50
Hounslow (Mdx), friars, 117
Hountenpath, John de, 18
Huish Champflower, 33; r of, see Burgh; rectory house, 121
Huish Episcopi, 78; v of, 32n
Hulle: Sir Edward, 21, 61, 102; Eleanor, 61–2; Elizabeth, wife of Robert, 126; Robert, 125–6; Thomas, 54
Hummer, see Trent
Hundon, Thomas, v of Chard, 126
Hungary, king of, 118
Hungerford: Walter, Lord, 86; family, 70, 103
Hunte, William, and his first wife Margaret, 55
Huntingdon: Anne, countess of, 100; earl of, 96
Huntspill: chapel, 122; r of, see Cogan
Huscarl, Alexandra, 126
Husee, James, 126
Husewyfe, Roger, 62
Hutton, r of, see Pykeslegh, Warcup
Hymmerford, John and his wife Joan, 126

Iceland: Holar, bp of, 86
Ide, Eleanor, 46; Thomas, 46

Idstock, chapel, 86
Iford, John, prior of Bath, 39
Ilchester, 68–9, 75; churches, 28, 75–6; gaol, 76; Whitehall, 22, 37, 75, 104
Ilminster, 47
Ilton: Merifield, chapel, 120; prebend, 109
Inge, Sir John, 126
Innocent VIII, pope, 113
Ireland, 37, 100; and see Dublin, Killala, Meath
Irisch (Irissch): Juliana, 54; Joan le, 54; Margery, 54, 126–7; Walter le, 54
Isaac, John, canon of Taunton, 20
Isabella, queen, 94

Jacob, Martin and his wife Joan, 21, 127
Jerard, John, and his wife Joan, 127
Jerusalem, 110
John XXII, pope, 108–9, 111
Julius II, pope, 110
Julius III, pope, 113
Jumieges (France), abbey, 96
Jurdayn, John, 48
Juyn (Joyn), Elizabeth, 62; Sir John, 62, 76

Katherine, of Aragon, queen, 105
Katherine, servant, 21
Keche, Jn, r of Sock Dennis, 3
Keel, Humphrey de, 127
Kelston, r of, see Barton
Ken, Elizabeth, wife of John de, 127
Kene, Hugh, 21
Keneley, chapel, 117
Kenn, 127; chapel, 117
Kenne: Jn, 127; Richard, 62
Kent, see Greenwich, West; Rochester
Kewstoke, Milton chapel, 54
Keynsham, 69, 72; abbey, 37–8, 69; abbot of, 72; Chewton Keynsham chapel of Holy Cross, 72; church, 54; new Lady Chapel at abbey, 58
Killala (Ireland), bp of, 87
Kilmersdon, 72; Coleford, chapel, 66, 72; Luckington, chapel in, 131; v of, 131
Kilmington (Som, now Wilts), r of, see Ludeford
Kilve, church, 85
King: John, 77; Oliver, bp of Bath & Wells, 50, 75, 80, 90, 105; register, 13
Kingsbury Episcopi, 18, 68, 82; chapel, 8; v of, 35
Kingsdon, 18, 71
Kingsteignton (Devon), bridge, 117
Kingston Seymour, 55, 65, 82
Kingston St Mary, 55; Tetton, oratory in, 122
Kingstone, 42, 71
Kittisford, Greenham, chapel in, 124; r of, 11
Knocston, Sir John, 63
Knyght: John, 45n; William, bp of Bath & Wells, 39, 91, 106
Knygth, John, 127
Kooper, Robert, 19
Kymyngton, Maud de, 54
Kynardeley, William, canon of Wells, 127

La Hogue (France), 96
Lambrook, Mr William, 63
Lambyn, John, 21
Lamplo (Langplo), Hugh or Henry, 53
Lancashire, see Lancaster, Liverpool
Lancaster, Thomas of, earl of Lancaster, 117
Langebrok, Robert and his wife Christian, 127
Langebrugge, Hugh de, 127
Langley (Wilts), 45
Langley, Katherine, 58

Langport, 47, 78; bridge, 117; hospital, 117; v of, 32n; Westover (Suthwyk, Frog Lane), 78
Lannoy, John, 127
Laverstoke, Geoffrey, 60
Lawher, Thomasia, 19
Lawrence, John, 58
Legyr, Roger, 128
Leicestershire, see Bosworth
Leigh, see Crowcombe
Leigh on Mendip, 50
Lewys, William, 50
Limington (Lymington), manor at, 132
Lincoln, Christina de, 63
Lincoln, bp of, 37, and see Repingdon; diocese, 5
Liverpool (Lancs), chapel, 117
Locking, r of, 4
Lodhuish, (Lodehiwissch) John de, 128
Lodhuish, see Nettlecombe
London, 2–3, 11, 16, 50–1, 64, 79- 80, 93, 99, 103, 105; bp of, 16; and see Gilbert; Carmelites' chapel, 63; diocese, 100; St Clement Dane, 79; St Paul's, 104; St Paul's, dean of, 50; St Thomas of Acon, hospital, 117; Temple Bar, 104; Tower, 96, 103–4; tradesmen, 81
Longley, William de, 64
Lottesham, William de, 130
Lottisham, see Ditcheat
Love, Katherine, 50
Luccombe, Geoffrey de, 128
Luccombe, 19; chantry in court, 128
Luckington, see Kilmersdon
Ludeford, William de, registrar, r of Kilmington, 13
Ludelowe, William de, v of Compton Bishop, 63
Ludes, Robert de, 128

Lugwardyn, John, canon and succentor of Wells, 63
Lutleton, 128
Lutleton, Mr William de, precentor of Wells, 128
Luttrell: John and his wife Joan, 128; Sir John, 53; Margaret, 53, 55
Lydeard St Lawrence, 104, 122; r of, 35, 122; and see Drayton
Lydeneye, Joan, 54
Lydford, West, 100; church, 86
Lymington, chantry, 104
Lympsham, church, 86
Lyvedod (Lyvedon), Roger, 63

Maister, John, 63
Malet: Sir Baldwin, lord of Enmore, and his wife Avice, 128; Margaret, see Eorul
Malherbe, William de, 128
Malvern, Little (Worcs), priory, 117
March, William of, bp of Bath & Wells, 7, 88–9, 110–11
Marchaunt, John, 128
Margaret, queen, 103
Mark, 83
Marlere, Robert le, 18
Marston Magna, ch, 6
Martel, Maud, 54
Martin V, pope, 112
Martock, 18, 21, 96, 105, 131; chapel, 123; lord of, see Fienles; Stapleton, chapel, 131
Martyn: Edmund, 128; Robert, 128
Mary, daughter of Edward I, 93
Mary, queen, 51, 107
Marys, John, and his wife Joan, 63–4
Massedy (Masseday), John, 60–1
Mathew, John, 64
Mayow, William, and his widow Agnes, 64
Meare, church, 85; r of, see Walter; v of, 68, 85

Meath (Ireland), bp of, see Yng
Mede, Philip, and his wife Isabel, 129
Meifolyne, Margaret, 45; and see Taunton, Andrew of
Melles, Philip, v of Wedmore, 32 and n
Mells, 54; r of, 46
Mendip Forest, 82
Meriet (Meryet): Sir John de, 64, 129; Simon de, 129
Merifield, chapel, 120
Merriott: chapel, 120; r of, see Papiti
Merssch (John in the), 18
Messingham, Robert de, prior of Taunton, 20
Micklefield (Yorks), 93
Middeltone, John de, r of Shepton Beauchamp, 59
Middeltone, chapel in, 127
Middlesex, see Chiswick
Midsomer Norton, 21
Milborne Port, Milborne Wick, 43; chapel in, 124; manor house, 125
Milton, see Kewstoke
Milverton, 55
Minchin Buckland, 36
Minehead, 19; Bratton, 120; v of, 68
Misterton, 69
Mohun: Ada de, wife of John de Mohun III, 64; Baldwin, 8; Payn, 64
Molesworth (Cambs), 93
Molton, Sir John de, 129
Molyneus, Robert, 118
Molyns, Robert, 125
Mone, John, 53, 56; Walter, 60
Monkton, West, 71, 106
Mont St Michel (France), abbey, 96
Montacute, 21, 23, 130; priory, 23, 36, 39, 110
Montague (Montacute, Montagu, Mountague): Alice, countess of Salisbury, 129; Elizabeth, countess of Salisbury, 22–4; John, earl of Salisbury, 23; John, 65; Katherine (nee Grandisson), countess of Salisbury, 23; Mary, 64; Robert, 25; Simon de, Lord, 22, 46; Thomas, earl of Salisbury, 24, 99; William (fl. 1255), 22; Sir William, Lord Montague, 22, 64; William, 1st earl of Salisbury, 23, 129; Wm, 2nd earl of Salisbury, 23; family 21, 24, 116
Montford, Henry de, r of Corton Denham, 5
Monthermer, Lord, 46
Moorlinch, 106
More, John atte, 129
Moreton (Morteone): Mr John, canon of Wells, 129; John and Alice, 129
Moretone, see Compton Martin
Moris, Sir J, 129
Morman, William, and widow Joan, 64
Mortimer, Roger de, earl of March, 94
Mottu (Motton), William, 118
Moulton, John, 129
Moureyt, prince of, 118
Muchelney: abbey, 37–9, 110, 115; abbot of, 48; prior of, 48; v of, 45
Mulburne, Sir William de, 129

Neroche, forest, chapel, 45
Nether Stowey, castle, 53
Nettlecombe, Lodhuish, oratory in, 128
Neville: Alice (nee Montague), countess of Salisbury, 24; Richard, earl of Salisbury, 24; Richard, earl of Warwick, 24, 104
Newcastle-upon-Tyne (Northumberland), 94

Newham, James, 19
Newton: Sir John, and his wife Isabel, 129; Ric, 63
Newton St Loe, chapel in, 132
Newton Surmaville, see Yeovil
Newyke or St Anne in the Woods (Glos), chapel, 69
Nicholas V, anti-pope, 111
Norfolk, see Norwich, Somerby
Normandy, 24
North, Mr William, v of North Curry, 130
Northamptonshire, see Fotheringhay, Peterborough
Northover, 68
Northumberland, see Newcastle-upon-Tyne
Norton Fitzwarren, 19
Norton St Philip, 49; chapel, 129; churchyard, 49
Norton sub Hamdon, 9, 71
Norwich (Norfolk), 99
Norys, Roger, 21
Nynehead, ch, 54
Nywelond, Robert and his wife Alice, 55

Oake, r of, see Thomas
Oare, r of, 46
Oath, see Aller
Odcombe, 23
Oke, Thomas, 49
Oldcastle, Sir John, 100
Oldelond, Robert de, 76
Ormond, Sir James, 76
Orum, Mr John, 60
Osbourn, Walter, v of Frome, 130
Othery, Thomasina, widow of Richard, 130
Otterton (Devon), priory, 95–6
Owle Knowle, see Carhampton
Oxford, 29–30, 75, 104; New Coll, 28
Oxstead (Surr), 80

Palton, Lady Elizabeth, 130
Papiti, Philip, r of Merriott, 110
Paris, 29
Passour, William, 58
Paulet, see Poulett
Pavely (Pauyle): Sir John de, 59; Sir Walter, 130
Pawlett, oratory, 130
Payne, John, r of Walton in-Gordano, 30
Pecock, Reginald, bp of Chichester, 49
Pedewel, Agnes, 130
Pendomer, r of, 7
Pennard, East, 72; Bradley, West, oratory, 128; Stone, chapel of St James, 72, 119n
Pensford (in Publow), 76; almshouse, 76; chapel, 76
Perceval (Percevall): James, 106; John le, 53
Percy, Henry (Hotspur), 98
Perry, see Quantoxhead
Person, John, younger, 118
Peter, v of Queen Camel, 130
Peterborough (Northants), abbey, 37
Petherton: North, 21, 127; Dunwear, chantry in, 133; Rhode, chapel, 131; v of, see Harowe;
Petherton, South, 28, 72
Peytevyn, William, and his wife Ellen, 54
Phelip (Richard), 18
Philip II, king of Spain, 107
Philip VI, king of France, 95–6
Pilton, v of, 6–7
Pipelpenne, oratory at, 128
Pirbright (Surr), 79
Pisa, Council, 111
Pitminster, 40, 69
Pittes, Richard, 15–16
Pitzpayn, Juliana, widow of Elias, 123

Plainsfield, see Stowey, Over
Plantagenet: Edward, earl of Warwick, 24, 104; Edward, prince of Wales, 103; George, duke of Clarence, 24, 103–4; Isabel (nee Neville), 24; Richard, duke of Gloucester, 103
Ploknet (Plokenet): Sir Alan, 65; Lady H de, 65; Sybil, 130
Plymstock, Richard de, 121
Poer, Henry, 130
Poitiers (France), 98
Poitou (France), 27
Poldens, 116
Pole: John atte (called le Smyth), 54; Sir John, 118; Margaret (nee Plantagenet), countess of Salisbury, 24; Reginald, abp of Canterbury, 107; Sir William, 24
Polsloe (Devon), priory, 6
Pomeroy, Alan, 3
Pontefract (Yorks), chapel, 117
Pope, Walter, 128
Porlock, 43, 56
Portbury, 58; Charlton, oratory, 131; church, 58; St Elyn's chapel, 58
Portishead, 48
Poteray, Thomas 55
Potyngthrop, see Banwell
Poulett (Paulet, Poulet): Amias, 80; Elizabeth, 130; John, 130
Powke, John, and his wife Annys, 58
Powncett, William, 20
Poytevyn, Richard, 59
Preste: John, 50; William, 59
Preston, see Yeovil
Price, Mr David, 100–01
Prowse, Thomas, prior of Taunton, 46
Publow, 35, 69, 76; curate of, 5; and see Pensford
Puckington, 104
Pucklechurch (Glos), 18, 58, 82

Puriton, 95; v of, 68
Putte, Stephen atte, r of Halse, 32
Puxton, church, 87–8
Pykeslegh: Adam, r of Hutton, 29; Roger de, r of Weston super Mare, 29; William, r of Backwell, 29
Pykman, John, archdeacon of Bath, 63
Pylle, r of, 71

Quantoxhead, East, 85; Perry, oratory at, 133
Quantoxhead, West, 68, 85
Queen Charlton, 69
Quinel, Peter, bp of Exeter, 27

Ralegh (Ralee), Joan de, 130; Joan de, widow, 130
Randolf, Sir John, 79
Redcliffe, Bristol, 50 and n; deanery, 33; St Katherine's chapel in St Mary's, 63; St Mary's church, 53, 62–3, 74, 87; parish, 50, 121, 129
Rede: John, 56; Thomas, 131
Redlynch, see Bruton
Reigni, John de, 131
Repingdon, Philip, bp of Lincoln, 47
Rew (Rewe), John, 21; another, 21
Reynolds, Walter, abp of Canterbury, 94
Rhode, see Petherton, North
Richard II, king, 98
Richard III, king, 104
Riphay, Agnes, 19
Ripon (Yorks), dean and chapter, 28
Robert I of Scotland (the Bruce), 93
Rochester (Kent): bridge, 117; diocese, 100
Rode, 61, 121; Charlton (Cherleton), manorial chapel, 121; r of, see White

Rodney: Sir John, 19; Richard, 79; Sir Walter and his wife Isabella, 131
Rodney Stoke, 82
Roland (Rowland), Mr John, canon of Wells, 61, 99n, 111–12, 131
Rome, 46, 110–11, 113; hospital, 117
Ronde, Thomas, 19
Rouen (France), 99
Roules, Adam, 27
Rowdon, see Stogumber
Rowley (Wittenham) (Wilts), 70
Ruishton, 69
Russell, Thomas, 58
Rypon, Richard de, 28
Ryuere, John de la, 131

Salisbury, earls of, see Montague; Neville
Salisbury (Wilts), 15–16, 77; bp of, 31; dean of, 110; diocese, 56, 70; St Osmund, pilgrimage, 49
Saltford, 19, 35; r of, 103
Sammell, John, 60
Sampford, Hugh and his wife Maud, 131
Samuel: Geoffrey, 131: Roger, canon of Taunton, 20; William, 131
Sandford Orcas (Som now Dors), 19; chapel in, 126
Saundford, William, 34
Saundres, Roger, 63
Say, Sir John, 131
Saymour, see Seymour
Schipham, Philip, 45
Schyrygge, Thomas de, and his wife Eleanor, 54
Scotland, 22, 93, 95–6, 106
Scoville, William de, 79
Seaborough (Som, now Dors.), 21, 25, 69; church, 86
Seavington St Michael, r of, see Attemede, Granden

Selwood, forest, 45
Selworthy: chapel in, 131; Holnicote, oratory, 130
Selyman, Robert, 53
Servyngton, Alys, 56
Seymour (Saymour), Millicent, 53; Roger and his wife Margaret, 131
Seynt John, Edward, 131
Seyntcler (Seyncler), Robert, 131
Shapwick, 71; church, 86
Shepton Beauchamp, r of, 32, and see Middeltone
Shepton Mallet, 19; r of, 104
Shepton Montague, v of, 68
Sherborne (Dorset), abbey, 65
Sherp, John, 131
Shipman, John, 50
Shoyll, John, prior of Bruton, 38–9
Shrewsbury (Salop), battle, 98
Shrewsbury, earl of, 102
Shrewsbury, Ralph of, bp of Bath & Wells, 3–4, 6, 13 and n, 18, 23, 26, 34, 37, 45–6, 58, 60 70, 74, 77, 79–80, 82, 88–9, 95, 97, 111; register, 8–9, 23, 81, 86, 89, 96–8; seals, 16
Sibley, John, 18
Sigismund, emperor, 112
Skelton (Yorks), 93
Skirlaw, Walter, bp of Bath & Wells, 9; register, 47
Slo, John atte, 131
Slough, see Curry, North
Smyth: (Richard le), 18; Thomas 56; Thomas (another), 64; William, 49; William, provost of Wells, 104
Sock Dennis, 104; r of, see Keche
Somerby (Norf), 118
Somerset, Aline, 56
Somerton, Robert of, 3
Somerton, gaol, 76
Sordyche, Edmund, 55
Southampton (Hants), 118
Spain, 118

Spaxton, manor ho, 126; r of, 32, and see Aleton
Spekyngton, Walter, and his father Thomas de, 46
Spenser, David, 60
Spere, Joan, 21
St Albans, battle, 102
St Anne in the Woods, see Newyke
St Clare, William de, 59
St Decumans, 68; v of, 71
Seyntlowe (Seynlo, Seynlowe, Seyntlou), Isabel, widow of Sir John, 56; John, 63; John (another), 132; John (another), 132; Sir John, 56; Sir Nicholas, 102
St Malo (France), 99, 118
Stafford: Humphrey, and his wife Isabel, 131; John, r of Farmborough, bp of Bath & Wells, abp of Canterbury, 4, 9, 13, 28–9, 38–9, 41–2, 47, 53, 63, 70, 76, 80, 86, 100–01, 112; register, 9, 47, 70
Standerwick (in Frome), 70; oratory in manor house, 128; r of, 70
Staplegrove, 69
Stapleton, Richard de, 54
Stapleton, see Martock
Stavordale, priory, 86, 117
Stawel, Eleanor de, 54
Stawley, Appley, 119
Sthaurachii, Sir John, 118
Stillington, Robert, bp of Bath & Wells, 38, 50, 80, 90, 103–4; register, 9–10, 90, 103, 113
Stockland Bristol, v of, 68
Stockwood, 69; church, 122; Rowdon, manor house, chapel, 130; Vexford, chapel in, 132
Stogursey, 105; priory, 21, 37, 95
Stoke St Gregory, Slough, 65
Stoke St Mary, 69
Stoke St Michael, 19, 72
Stoke sub Hamdon, 47; college, 21, 37, 103; oratory, 123; r of, 106

Stokes, Mr John, canon of Wells, 132
Storthwayt, John, registrar, 13–16
Stourton: John, 80, 86; Sir Reginald, 44, 56
Stowell, Robert, 21
Stowey, Nether, 95
Stowey, Over: Adscombe, chapel of St Mary, 61; Plainsfield, manor house, chapel, 132
Stowye, John, 19
Stradelyng, Elizabeth, widow of Edward, 132
Strange, John, 43
Stucle, Richard, 19
Sudbury, Richard de, 54
Sugar, Dr Hugh, 91
Surrey, see Oxstead, Pirbright, Walton on the Hill
Sutton: Sir John, 79; Richard, and his wife Alice, 132; William de, 132
Sutton Bingham, 71; r of, 71, and see Wylkyns
Sutton Montis, 21, 24, 26, 119
Sutton, Long, church, 87
Swainswick, r of, see Bath
Sydenham: Alice, 55; Henry and Richard, 132
Symond (Richard), 18
Syon (Mdx), abbey, 105

Talbot, John, 5
Tanner, Robert, 76
Taunton, Andrew of, 45; and see Meifolyne
Taunton, 19, 48, 55, 77, 124, 128; archdeacon of, 109; archdeacon of, seal, 11; archdeaconry, 7; canons of, 20, 43, and see Alresford, Columpstoke, Godalming, Isaac, Samuel; castle, chapel in, 131; deanery, 69; minster, 69; prior of, 40, 104, and see Messingham, Prowse;

priory, 37–9, 69, 110, 115;
St James's, 69; St Margaret's
hospital, 117; St Mary
Magdalene, 19, 34, 46, 69, 77,
96; chapel, 86; v of, see Dyssham
Taylor alias Cardmaker, John,
chancellor of Wells, v of
Wellington, 51
Tellisford, oratory, 130
Temple Newsham (Yorks), 93
Templecombe, preceptory, 39, 110
Tenos, bp of, see Cornish
Tetton, see Kingston St Mary
Teutebury, William, 54
Teynturer, Richard le, 75
Thomas, Brother, 45; r of Oake,
30; v of Clevedon, 59
Thomere (Richard le), 18
Thorncombe (Dors), 55; and see
Bicknoller
Thynne, Sir John, 9n
Timberscombe, 19
Timsbury, r of, see Bois
Tintinhull, 23; r of, 4
Todenham, Robert de, 132
Tornezete (Thomas de), 18
Towker, John, vicar choral of Wells
cathedral, 132
Towyn, Roger, 61
Trent (Som, now Dors), Hummer,
oratory in, 125
Trowe (Trew): John and his wife
Agnes, 132; Thomas, 132
Trull, 69
Tudor, Henry, duke of Richmond,
106
Turtle (Tertle), Roger, 54, 59
Twe, William, vicar choral of Wells
cathedral, 89
Tybryghton, Rog de, registrar, 13
Tylly: Leonard, and his wife Joan,
132; William, 21

Underhulle, Christiana, 54
Uphill, John, 21

Uphill, 19, 68; r of, 3
Urswick, Christopher, r of Chedzoy
Uske, John de, 59

Valde, Robert, 59
Vaughan, Henry, mayor of Bristol,
75
Vergil (or Castellen), Polidore,
archdeacon of Wells, 105
Vexford, see Stogumber
Vilate, Anthony, 21

Wadham: Edward, 56; J, and his
wife Isabel, 133; Katharine, 133
Wakefield (Yorks), 24
Walden (Essex), abbey, 93n
Wales, 22, 37, 55; Prince of, 31;
and see Coity, Goldcliff
Walshawe, Richard, 62
Walssh (Walissh, Walsche): John
(fl 1345), 57; John (fl 1446), 58;
John (fl 1499), 50; Thomas, 118
Walter: r of Exton, 29; r of Meare,
30
Walton, Petronilla, 133
Walton in Gordano, manor chapel,
121; r of, 30, and see Payne
Walton on the Hill (Surr), 79
Walwayn, John, 13
Warcop, Edmund, r of Hutton, 29
Warmwell, John, 127
Warre, John, 86
Warwyc, William de, Templar, 39
Warynner (Geoffrey le), 18
Wasyn, Thomas, 39
Watchet, harbour, 118
Watercombe, see Chard
Waterford (Ireland), bp of, 84–5
Wayford, 69
Weare, 54; chapel of St Thomas,
11; church, 86; Lower, 81
Wedmore, 82; Blackford, q.v.; v of,
32, and see Melles
Welles, Richard of, 74
Wellesleigh (in Wells), 18, 89

Wellington, 18, 34; chapel, 129; oratory in, 123; v of, see Taylor
Wellow, manor house, 121
Wells: Hugh of, bp of Lincoln, 6n; Jocelin of, bp of Bath & Glastonbury, 6 and n, 7, 67, 78
Wells: archdeacon of, 60, and see Cherlton, Holes, Vergil; archdeaconry, 7, 109
Wells: bishop's palace, 2, 43, 80–1; chapel, 50; chapel of St Mark, 81; keeper, see Cammel
Wells: cathedral, 6, 29, 31, 58, 60, 77–8, 81, 88–91, 95, 109; canons, 5, 50, 77, and see Canon, Frome, Kynardley, Lugwardyn, Moreton, Roland, Stokes, Sudbury; chancellor, 111, and see Cornish, Taylor; chapter, 109; chapter house, 47; cloister, 6; dean of, 7, 47, And see Godele; prebend, 29, and see Ilton, Wiveliscombe; precentor, 78, and see Lutleton; provost, see Smyth; Treasury, 11; vicars choral, 31, 89, and see Alampton, Bath, Gernesey, Towker, Twe
Wells: city, 2, 4, 11, 18–19, 21, 27, 30, 50–1, 53–4, 55, 64, 77, 82, 102, 110, 120–1, 123–4, 127, 130–2; charter, 77; Guildhall, 77; master, see Godewyn; manor, 89; Mountroy college, 61; St Andrew's well, 78; streets, 49, 77; tradesmen, 77; Vicars' Close, 61, 90, 132
Wells: churches and chapels: St Cuthbert's, 34–5, 60–1, 86–7; curate, 56; v of, 5, and see Frome; St John's hospital, 11, 38, 61, 67, 78, 115; St Mary by the Cloister, 90; St Thomas's, 77; Vicars' Close, 90, 132
Wells, and see Dulcote, Easton, Wellesleigh

Wellyngton, Robert, 124
Wembdon, church, 85; St John's spring, 43
Weryngton, 55
Westbury, 82; v of, 53
Westbury-on-Trym (Glos), college, 31
Westerleigh (Glos), 79
Westminster, abbey, 63, 100
Weston Bampfylde, 21, 24–5
Weston super Mare, r of, see Pykeslegh
Westover, see Langport
Weyhill (Hants), 93
Wherwell, Walter de, 3
White: John, r of Rode, 61; Nicholas, 50; Patrick, registrar, 13
Whitelackington, 120, 133; and see Ffrie
Whiteman, Joan, 62
Whityngton, John de, 54
Wick St Lawrence, 27; church, 85–6
Wike, see Wyke
Wild, Richard le, 133
Wille, Isabel, 55
William, Brother, 47
Williamson, Robert, registrar, 6, 13
Wilton, 69
Wiltshire, 28; and see Goatacre, Heytesbury, Rowley, Salisbury
Winchester (Hants), 118; College, 28; diocese, 20
Windsor (Berks), 104; St George's chapel, 104
Winford, 19, 35
Winscombe, 45, 82; chapel, 54; v of, 54; Winterhead, oratory, 120; Woodborough, chapel, 120
Winsford, 67–8; v of, 68
Winsham, La Heighe, chapel in, 125
Winterstoke, hundred, 82, 94

Witham Friary, 36; chapel, 87; priory, 36, 111
Witheridge (Devon), r 32
Withiel, see Cannington
Withycombe: chapel in, 128; church, 122; manor, 122
Withypool, 66
Wittecomb, William, 118
Wiveliscombe, 4, 8, 11, 20, 60, 80, 97; Allery, chapel in, 122; chapel, 80; church, 64; prebend, 109; v of, 67
Wode, Richard atte (or Compton), 8
Wolsey, Thomas, abp of York, bp of Bath & Wells, 38, 106, 110, 113
Woodspring, priory, 37–8, 85, 115
Woodwick, 66, 70
Wookey, 61, 71, 80, 82; Bleadney, 116; chapel, 80
Woolavington, 68, 95
Wootton Courtenay, 19
Worcester: bp of, 31; diocese, 12n, 30, 47, 117
Worcestershire see Malvern, Little
Worm, John, 45
Wraxall, Birdcombe, house at, 129
Wrington, 50, 72; Burrington, chapel, 87; Bourne, 120
Wyatt, Sir Thomas, 107
Wycliffe, John, 47–8, 75
Wydecomb, see Corston
Wyke (Wike), Agnes, 54; John, de, 54, 133

Wyke, see Compton Dando, Yatton
Wyke Champflower, 45–6
Wylkyns, Hugh, r of Sutton Bingham, 30
Wymyate, Peter atte, 133
Wynd (William), 19
Wytcombe, Richard, 50
Wytham, Roger de, r of Donyatt, 65

Yarlington, 21–4; r of, 22
Yatton, 68, 82; chapel, 54; Wyke, oratory at, 133
Yenston, John, 133
Yenston, see Henstridge
Yeovil, 3, 34, 78, 105, 118, 125; almshouse, 78; chantries, 78; Newton Surmaville, chapel in, 127; oratory, 122; Preston, manor, chapel in, 133
Yeovilton, r of, 46, 89
Yng (Inge), Dr Hugh, v of Wellow, bp of Meath, abp of Dublin, 110
Yonge (Zonge): Alice, widow of William, 55; John le, Alice his widow, Miles his son, 65; Thomas, 48, 50; William le, 3
York, Edward, duke of, 100
York, 7, 93–4; abp of, 28, 98; diocese, 5
Yorkshire, see Micklefield, Skelton, Pontefract, Temple Newsham, Wakefield, York

Zonge see Yonge